ATHLETES on the STUMP and the STAGE

DR. JAMES E. HOLBROOK

ISBN: 1496086945
ISBN 13: 9781496086945
HOLBROOK, JAMES E.
ATHLETES ON THE STUMP AND THE STAGE

TABLE OF CONTENTS

PREFACE

Several trivia books have been written about sport, and many others have been written about politicians and entertainers. However, few have been written concerning the athletic backgrounds of politicians and entertainers. While the information is not hard to find, the difficulty is when one tries to make the needed associations. One might hear that a congressman graduated from a particular university and later see an interview during an election campaign that he/she was a college athlete in a particular sport. Then you have two pieces of information that can be connected in order to state that your congressman played quarterback for the football team at that university. After hearing several of these interviews, you may find that several of your congressmen were either teammates or competed against some of your favorite entertainers. As a sport management professor, I have always been interested in this type of information. When others told me that they enjoyed reading about that type of information as well, I decided to write this book. If you have read college yearbooks or sports rosters and found names and/or photos of congressman and/or entertainers, you know what I mean. For this reason, I spent a lot of time trying to decide whether or not to include a bibliography for most of this material. Since so much of the material is readily available, it becomes an issue of how many citations will appear in the text, and which citation of the same information should be used. Since most of the material is either common knowledge or information heard from many different sources, including watching the celebrity play ball at a live game, there is no need to include a list of references for that type of material. However, a reader usually wants to read another source where that information can be found. Therefore, my selected reference list includes some referenced material as well as some of the other sources where material about the celebrities in this book can be found. Although most of the information concerning congressmen can be found in other sources, I chose senate.gov and house.gov for most of these citations. The key to this book is making all of the relationships and associations about these celebrities in the form of quizzes and puzzles found in chapters 4, 5, 6, and 7. You will find out that some of your favorite entertainers were teammates with, or competed against your congressmen. You will also find out that many of your congressmen were teammates, and many more of your favorite entertainers were also teammates, and there was an obvious reason that so many of your favorite action movies included many of these former athletes. There are many stories and quizzes about entertainers who played in movies with other celebrities discussed in this book. In some of the quizzes you may read some similar information that you read in another quiz. Since many of the older TV and movie stars were multi sport athletes, they may appear in multiple categories. For example, western TV and movie star Dale Robertson was an eight sport college athlete. Sport trivia about many more of your favorite celebrities are written in this book. I hope you find the material, as well as the quizzes and puzzles enjoyable.

INTRODUCTION

Many of us have watched the movie, Field of Dreams. It was a very passionate movie about athletes, specifically, famous professional baseball players from the past, who appear in a farmer's corn field in Iowa to play the game they loved so well when they were alive. Not being a movie producer, I can only imagine the kind of passion that was felt by the cast, when they were chosen to star in this movie. Many of them were former athletes, themselves. The star of the movie, Kevin Costner, was a former college baseball player for one of the best teams in the NCAA. It is no fluke that Costner has been offered so many roles when the leading man was a baseball player. He is a member of a distinguished club of actors in Hollywood. These are actors who are former athletes. "Athletic grace" is difficult to fake. While many actors may be physically fit, they will have difficulty performing as an athlete or a coach if they have never experienced this unique phenomenon. I remember watching a film about how this movie was made. When people at the movie site met Kevin for the first time, they said that he had played baseball in college and seemed to know what he was doing.

Many studies have revealed the amazingly high percent of men that really think they should have played professional sports. However, a recent poll, of the top ten most difficult activities in sport, revealed that hitting a baseball traveling 90 miles per hour was the most difficult of these activities. However, this action is one that many people think they could achieve. This is because great athletes make it look easy. However, if the average man tries to hit a ball, at that speed, he will discover that it is quite difficult. Without listing the many factors that make this feat unrealistic, the average person simply does not have a fast enough reaction time to "check the ball", or more importantly, hit one, in the "strike zone". This is the most important factor when baseball scouts are analyzing a potential player. A pitcher can simply throw bad pitches all day to someone who does not possess the basic physical abilities to play baseball.

For actors like Kevin Costner, "athletic grace" is an occurrence that appears whenever he plays the role of a baseball player. As a former college baseball player, Costner has been required to train thousands of hours throwing as well as hitting a baseball traveling at various velocities, and with various throwing patterns. While a former college baseball player, like Costner, can also make this feat look easy, it is quite difficult.

Costner was not the only athlete in Field of Dreams. The actor who played the role of Kevin's brother-in-law was Timothy Busfield, a semi-professional baseball player. However, Timothy did not get the opportunity to play ball in the movie. We could list other athletes in the movie, as well. However, a major theme of this book is probably best characterized by the character played by one of the greatest athletes in the history of Hollywood. Burt Lancaster, a former circus performer, played Dr. Archibald "Moonlight" Graham, a former professional baseball player, who played one game of major league baseball, in 1922 and returned to his hometown in Minnesota, to become a doctor.

In the movie, Kevin Costner, plays an Iowa farmer that has been given the ability to talk to baseball players that had been dead for many years. When he goes searching for Dr. Archibald Graham, he discovers that he had been dead for 16 years. However, Dr. Graham's neighbors and former patients told him stories about the great things he had done as a doctor, in his hometown. One evening, Costner's character is transported back to the year 1972, and meets the ghost of Dr. Graham, as an old man. After discussing Dr. Graham's story, about himself as a young man, whose only regret was that he did not get the chance to bat, during his one game in major league baseball, Costner's character tried to convince him to come to Iowa and re-live his dream, stating how important it is to get that opportunity, even if it only occurred for five minutes. Dr. Graham replied that the real tragedy would have been if he had only been a doctor for five minutes. Terrence Mann (played by James Earl Jones) explained that if Archie Graham had received his time at bat, and got a hit, he may have stayed in baseball, and there would have been no Dr. Graham. However, when Costner's character is driving back to Iowa, Dr. Graham's ghost returns as a young Archie "Moonlight" Graham, to play the game again. After one time at bat, a child watching the game is injured, and the young Archie Graham, realizes the importance of his other "calling". He gives up his ability to remain a young man, on the ball field, and steps out into our world, as a much older, Dr. Graham, in order to save the child's life. No one from an athletic background could have fought back the tears during this scene. It was well done and the moment lives on as a monument to athletes who have sacrificed their own wants and desires for another "calling".

Some of the greatest success stories in many different professions have developed when great athletes recognized another "calling", and used characteristics they developed as athletes to perfect their talents in other parts of their lives. In a time when some of the media often portray negative activities of a few athletes, it is important to remember that most athletes are good role models that either become great role models as professional and Olympic athletes and/or recognized other ways to use characteristics derived from sports, in other parts of their lives. For example, a few years ago, the winner of the Heisman trophy was professional football player, Tim Tebow. As the first sophomore to win this prestigious award, Tim spent much of his free time doing missionary work. While most football fans probably expected Tim to remain a professional football player, he could become a minister, or like Kyle Rote Jr. (a former professional soccer player and Episcopal minister), a professional athlete and a minister.

One might wonder what must have been going through Burt Lancaster's mind as he played the role of Dr. Archibald Graham. I find it unique that he was playing someone so similar to himself. Burt Lancaster had been a great athlete that was much older, now. At nearly 80, this would be one of his last performances. Not long after the movie, he died. However, before he died, he spent some time in a coma. While being interviewed on a talk show, Kirk Douglas, a great college wrestler, who became a famous actor, said that it was difficult to watch Burt lay in a coma. He explained that Burt had been one of the best athletes he had ever worked with. As a former trapeze artist, in the circus, he could do his own stunts in action roles, in which most people would have thought to be set up with stuntmen. Like so many athletes-turned-actor, a hand injury ended Lancaster's career as a circus performer. While such an injury did not keep him from becoming a great stuntman in Hollywood, it could have been fatal as a circus performer.

I remember watching the movie, The Crimson Pirate, for the first time, and being amazed at some of the stunts Burt (as a young man) performed during this movie. Being from another generation, I asked my mother about this actor. She explained how Burt Lancaster had been a great athlete and "sex symbol" for her generation. In movies where other actors had to get a stuntman to perform the major action parts, Burt had no problem performing his own stunts. In one movie, he actually played a circus performer. In another role, he played Jim Thorpe, one of the greatest athletes of all time. Only another athlete could portray Thorpe, so well. Although, he never played the role of Tarzan, in the movies, during the 1960s, when the film industry was searching for a new athletic-actor to play the role, it was said that they were looking for a younger version of Burt Lancaster.

ATHLETES ON THE STUMP AND THE STAGE

Mr. Lancaster has given enjoyment to many people who watched these movies, over the years. By using his talents to bring such roles to the movies, the world changed in a positive way. This is very much like the character he played in Field of Dreams. I do not know how many lives Archibald Graham saved when he chose to become a doctor, but I am quite certain that his background as an athlete was a great asset.

As a college professor of sport management, I have researched this premise. Often, when successful people have been interviewed, they attributed the qualities they gained from their athletic backgrounds, as major contributors to their success. Several studies have illustrated the advantages of competing in sport. Many studies illustrate that high school athletes actually made significantly better grades than non-athletes. Many reasons are given for this occurrence. Athletes learn how characteristics such as discipline, confidence, drive, motivation, patience and teamwork "pay off" when they achieve their perspective goals. People who insist on portraying athletes as "dumb jocks" have, apparently, not seen the long list of names that make up the Academic All-Americans in our nation's colleges and universities, or another list of athletes that were named Rhodes Scholars. They are probably not aware of the annual list of the top academic-athletic programs in the NCAA and NAIA, as well. However, we should probably refer to these athletes by the way their talents were applied to their career in politics, or the stage, and how athletics helped to shape their personality to be the successful men and women we know and admire.

During a program on ESPN, former U.S. Presidents were interviewed, giving their opinions on how football helped to shape their lives. Presidents Reagan and Ford were very vocal concerning the discipline and motivation needed to achieve a higher level of performance and how it helped them to understand their responsibilities as President of the United States.

President Gerald Ford had been an All-American at the University of Michigan. He was offered positions to play professional football for the Green Bay Packers, as well as the Detroit Loins. However, he chose to turn it down and coach football and boxing at Yale University, while he went to law school. Normally, law students are not allowed to have full time jobs. However, Ford not only attended law school while working as a full time coach, he graduated near the top of his class. Shortly after graduating, and becoming a successful lawyer, World War II began. While he was not required to join the military, he volunteered, and was a decorated naval officer. Like Archibald Graham, he had a different calling after having the opportunity to be a professional athlete. In fact, President Gerald Ford has one of the most impressive resumes in our history. Everything he did, during his life, seemed to lead to success. Then he became President of the United States, during one of the most difficult periods in our history. Again, he performed admirably.

President Ronald Reagan's life was very similar. He not only played football for Eureka College, in Illinois, he was also the captain of his swimming team. After graduating, he became a sportscaster, followed by many years as a major movie icon. After many years as a movie star, he became the governor of California, followed by a two-term President of the United States, winning more states in his second election than any other president in history.

California Congressman Bob Mathias was arguably the greatest athlete of all time. He is the only American to win two Olympic gold medals in the decathlon. In the 1948 Olympics, he won the gold medal in the decathlon, when he was only 17 years old. Four years later, he led Stanford University's football team to the Rose Bowl. He was recruited by the Washington Redskins, but turned it down (USAToday.com, 2006, September 3). Later, that year, he said that he would not return to the Olympics because he was getting married and preparing for medical school. However, his

6

home town of Tulare, California was counting on him to defend his title, and his fiancé said she would wait for him. He not only competed in the 1952 Olympics, he became the spokesman for the Games. The decathlon is ten track events, performed over a two day period. During the second event, he pulled a muscle in his thigh. When someone asked if he was dropping out, he said he was still going to win, as he did. After the Olympics, he finished college, while starring in two movies, after which he served in the Marines. Afterward, he starred in other movies and during the 1960s, he became a U.S. Congressman. Many years later, during an interview, he jokingly, stated that so many things happened after the 1952 Olympics that he never got the chance to attend medical school. Bob died a few years ago, leaving a legacy of a man that put his whole heart into everything he did. Like President Ford, he was a man that worked hard to accomplish his athletic goals, and moved on to compete in other pursuits after he reached them. I could probably write a book about Bob Mathias. I have a movie about his life, and I have almost met him. As a young track athlete beginning to train for the decathlon, I attended the opening for the Track & Field Hall of Fame. Although, many of the athletes from previous Olympics were present, I was mostly impressed by Bob Mathias. Although, I passed him in the hall, I asked the assistant director for the Hall of Fame to introduce me. However, as we were on our way to meet Mr. Mathias, the lights were turned off for the evening entertainment, and I did not get the chance to meet him.

There are many other athletes who chose to serve society in a variety of ways, other than sport. Many of them served in the U.S. Congress, as well as the Senate, and some of them became President of the United States. In 2004, CBC Sports Online developed a list of the top ten athletes, who became politicians in various countries. Four of them were Americans (CBC.CA, 2004, May 14).

Many of our favorite entertainers came from an athletic background, as well. Many of them continue to compete in sport. Golf Digest often lists the top players in Hollywood (2005, December). Some of these athletes were preparing for another calling, while others left the sports arena for other reasons, such as an injury. Regardless of the reason, our society has gained from their choice.

This book will inform its readers of many celebrities and politicians who have made the choice to pursue a career outside of the coliseum. Some of them are well known athletes that have progressed through life and challenged themselves in other areas of their life. While many people think that being a successful athlete is all anyone should aspire, many athletes view sport as only one way to reach their goals. When they have reached all of their goals in sport, it is time to reach their goals in other areas of their life. However, most of the celebrities in this book are individuals who are not well known as athletes. They are more like Dr. Graham, and President Ford. Sport had shaped their lives in order to make them the congressman, musician or actor we know today. Readers may be surprised to find out how much their favorite entertainers had in common with their congressman, and with each other. The second half of this book will illustrate some of these interesting comparisons. Some of them may be quite obvious, but never published, while others may be a complete surprise.

While one may not be surprised to discover that President Ronald Reagan and Governor Arnold Swartzeneggar have each been athletes, movie stars, and the Governor of California, they may be surprised to discover a congressman from California was considered to be the "World's Greatest Athlete". One may be surprised to discover that Congressman Jim Ryun went to college on the same type of athletic scholarship as the actors Bill Cosby and Michael Landon. While Michael Landon grew up on the east coast, and may have had no idea that he would soon be a movie star, when he moved to California, on a USC track scholarship, pop musician Chuck Negron, of Three Dog Night (also from the east coast), intentionally, turned down other basketball scholarships, to accept the one offered to him in California, in order to enhance his music career. A TV and move star who strongly identifies with the content of this book would be a four-sport college athlete named Kevin Sorbo, who, in taped interviews, told the story of going to college as a champion athlete and discovering that his college teammates were champions as well, calling home to tell his dad about his concerns as a career athlete. Today, as a well-known movie star he is a champion who teaches children through his foundation to excel in all areas of their lives.

The sources of this book are quite unique. Some of them were TV interviews such as those you may have heard on Johnny Carson, while others were narrative information such as those from Robert Osborne when he spoke about the background of actors on Turner Classic Movies. One unique way I discovered, was through searching through several college yearbooks and sports rosters for celebrities that I knew were college athletes. Another source is simply watching a lot of movies which co-starred many of the professional athletes we have watched in various sports, therefore, needing no reference. While I am sure that some of the material about celebrities named in this book can be found in other books, Wikipedia.org, IMDb.com, Biographies.com, Starpulse.com, House.gov, Senate.gov, and personal websites, the bulk of this material is a culmination of years of researching books, directories, magazine articles, talk shows, biographies, documentaries, websites, interviews with friends of celebrities, as well as first person knowledge. Although, I have included a bibliography that includes several personal websites, such as those from Congressmen and Senators, many of these celebrities have multiple sources where this information can be found. There was no need to site references for congressmen who were professional or Olympic athletes such as Steve Largent or Bob Mathias because they were nationally and internationally known athletes with hundreds of references concerning their athletic background. For the same reason, there was no need to site references for many of the movie stars and musicians who were well known athletes with many references of information about their athletic backgrounds. Although, most of the material in this book can be found through many sources, I have found no book that includes a cumulative collection of this material. More importantly, most of this book is made up of games, puzzles and trivia about these celebrities in a way that no book has ever been published. The material began as a way for the author to tell related stories to his sport management classes, in an attempt to make lectures more interesting. After several years of gathering material from various sources, friends and other professors suggested that it would be the kind of book they would enjoy reading. I hope you will enjoy it too.

CHAPTER 1

BRIDGING HISTORY TO SPORT AND SOCIETY

When we look at the history of sport we find a much different picture than what is proposed in some of the media events on television that seem to concentrate on the few athletes that have social problems. However, sport is a microcosm of society. If one percent of men in America are in prison, we may find that one percent of male athletes are in prison, as well. However, the vast majority of athletes are respectable men and women, and great role models for children. Throughout history, sport has been a major force in our lives, representing people who were disciplined, confident, motivated people with a superior work ethic.

The Olympic Games originated in Ancient Greece. The Greeks viewed sport as a religious experience. It was a symbol of their society. Forbes (cited in Romano, 1972), explained the many uses of the Greek palestra, literally meaning "place of wrestling." He indicated that the custom of daily exercise and a bath brought men to the building, and once there in the company of their fellows, they found that there was no better place for social interaction, small talk, relaxation, lounging, dissemination of news and views, and serious conversation and discussion. This is very similar to the sports club atmosphere of today.

The sophists of the late fifth century B.C. used some of the rooms facing the interior courtyard of the palestra as lecture halls (Romano, 1972). There could be a philosopher teaching at one end of the palestra while an athletic event was taking place in the courtyard. In fact, lots of these philosophers were athletes, themselves. For example, Plato, one of the most famous philosophers in ancient history was a champion wrestler. This reality makes it quite amusing when modern aristocrats with a purely cognitive disposition, talk of Plato as if he were a wimp. If they were to investigate, they would find that Plato was not his given name. It was a name given to him because of his physique. Plato means "broad shoulders." We could make a list of other famous philosophers and scientists to find many of them, such as Aristotle and Archimedes were also wrestlers. The Ancient Greeks believed in a concept called arete', which means striving for perfection mentally, as well as physically. Although, the Greeks are known for their philosophical views toward life, in general, athletics and physical exercise were just as important.

In Medieval Europe, social class was often determined by the classification of sport practiced. The wealthy participated in "court sports," such as fencing, while the poor participated in "garden sports", such as wrestling. During the early part of American society, before there were many organized sport associations, men would challenge each other to wrestling and boxing tournaments in pubs, or the local area. One such man in Illinois, named Lincoln was best known as a wrestler when he lived in an area that is now a part of Indiana. Abraham, at 6'4" and strong, 190 years ago would have been like a 6'10" wrestler today (White, cited in WWE.com). While Abraham was a tall, slender man who did not resemble most wrestlers, Lincoln became a champion professional wrestler. He was also known for shaking hands with his opponent, afterwards. Of course, young Abraham did not become a celebrity with the WWE. However, he did manage to become the sixteenth president of the United States.

In today's society, people often want to know why athletes compete in sport. The only people who think it is easy are people who have never competed against good competitors. Why would someone compete in something that is so hard? If it is for a scholarship, there are much easier ways to pay for college. If it is for fame, there are easier ways to become famous. If it is about money, there are easier ways to make money. However, athletes overcome many obstacles in order to train long, hard hours, under the worst of conditions. According to Ostro (cited in Holbrook, 1997), the controversy over Proposition 42 had caused coaches to respond in a variety of ways. Coach Thompson's dramatic "walk" concerning Proposition 42 induced the NCAA to reconsider the rule. However, professional tennis player Arthur Ashe asserted that every time educational standards changed, athletes got the message. While many people underestimated these athletes, they did what was necessary to pass the standards to compete.

In a survey conducted by the Athletic Footwear Association (cited in Holbrook, 1997), over ten thousand boys and girls were asked the most important reasons for participating in organized sport. The undisputed reason was "to have fun". When they were asked why they no longer competed, it was because they "lost interest". Many people have competed in sport for many reasons. Some did it "for the love of the game." Others found it to be a "stepping stone" to other careers. Former boxing champion, Sugar Ray Robinson once explained that while he did not necessarily like to box, he liked the results of winning. According to Coakley (2004), there are six sociological theories of sport, and at least one of them (functionalist theory) describes sport as an essential part of American culture, with many preconceived ideas for conduct. The conclusions about the sport-society relationship, concerning this theory states that sport is a valuable social institution that benefits society as well as individuals in society.

One of the generally accepted educational content areas of sport management is called sport ethics. This course studies the ethical values placed on sport and its heroes. Although, some athletes have remarked that they do not want to be role models for children, they are, whether they like it or not. A biography about Mickey Mantle illustrated how children learned how to work math problems by calculating Mantle's batting average. Sport is a big part of our society and famous athletes do not have the luxury of declining their responsibility as a role model. If athletes are not a positive role model, children may mimic them anyway, and cause problems for their parents and society. Fortunately, most athletes are very good role models.

One trade where we find many former athletes in our society is politics. On the surface it might seem odd that politicians would have the same qualities as athletes, given the political environment of some athletic events. Recently, the International Olympic Committee (IOC) was criticized for choosing Beijing, China as the site for the 2008 Olympics. Regardless, of their political views, they can not "boycott" an Olympic site for political reasons. Disapproval of a country's view of human rights kept the Soviet Union out of the Olympics until 1952. The International Olympic Committee realized that it was against their own rules to omit them. Therefore, the IOC could not support the United States when they boycotted the 1980 Olympics in Moscow. Likewise, they did not support the Soviet Union when they boycotted the 1984 Olympics in Los Angeles. Some elements of our society tend to judge participation in sport based on their own views. However, athletes usually have a different viewpoint. They gain a deep respect for others that compete well, regardless of their political views.

Athletes tend to rise above political disputes, during athletic competitions. There are many examples of athletes becoming friends under the worst of political circumstances. Athletes tend to look beyond political views to find friends at athletic events. A good example was recorded during the 1936 Olympics, in Berlin. Although, Hitler could not stand to watch Jesse Owens win four gold metals, Owens had no trouble becoming friends with his German rival, in the long jump. They actually helped each other to compete well in the event. During the 1976 Olympics, Mac Wilkins, the American who won the gold medal in the discus was seen hugging Wolfgang Schmidt, the silver medalist from East Germany. Although, this is very common among athletes, some Americans expressed their political opinions about Wilkins. This did not shake Wilkins ideal of competition, or his friendship with fellow discus throwers from other countries.

Mutual respect among athletes is not a new concept. The original Olympics were often fought between Greek communities that were at war with each other. But during the Olympics they were not allowed to fight. And after the Olympics were completed, they would return to their battle. Most athletes seem to gain this very positive quality. They can express respect for other athletes, even when they are enemies.

Perhaps the most misunderstood story in sport was that of boxing champions Max Schmeling and Joe Louis. This was before and during WWII, and fans thought the worst of their hero's opponent. As the German boxing champion, Max was actually accused of being a Nazi. However, the movie entitled Max and Joe revealed that Max actually risked his life to aid people to escape punishment from the Nazi occupation. Max and Joe were very good friends who had the deepest respect for each other. Politicians who are former athletes often use the lessons they learned in sport to help them make important decisions for our country. This quality should give them an advantage when dealing with people that have opposing political views. One good example was that of Senator Bill Bradley and Senator Jack Kemp. Although, they were members of different political parties, they were two former professional athletes with a deep respect for each other who worked well together in the U.S. Senate.

Governments generally have a vested interest in maintaining the idea that success is based on discipline, loyalty, determination and the ability to keep working in the face of hardship and bad times. Some countries view sport as a sense of friendship and collectivism, while others, like the United States associate the image of sport competition with success and hard work. It is not surprising that so many members of the federal government began their road to success, with sports. It is unfortunate that so few of these athletes remain in our government.

While Coakley explains there are six major theories that apply to sport, two of the contrasting views are the functionalist theory and the conflict theory. The functionalist theory ascribes that "sport is a valuable social institution, which benefits society as well as individuals in society." Conflict Theory states that "sport is a form of physical activity that is distorted by the needs of capital" (Coakley, 2004). Researchers in conflict theory tend to focus on the possibility that organized sport may alienate children from sport. However, researchers in functionalist theory are more focused on how to keep the child in a sport that teaches him/her positive lessons attributed to the sport. On the other hand, some athletes, as well as administrators may view either of these theories to be correct and recognize the value of sport. We have heard the famous comedian/actor/educator Bill Cosby say that he ran track to go to college, he did not go to college to run track. While Dr. Cosby appears to have a love of sport, he also saw it as a unique opportunity to acquire an education that has served him well. Besides making a fortune, he also has a doctorate degree in education.

Many young people view sport as a way to acquire financial stability. If their goals are realistic, this is not a bad thing. We have witnessed many successful individuals that had a relatively short sports career before they attained success in another part of their life. Some of these athletes may have longed to make this change. However, others may have wanted a long career in sport and recognized a better opportunity in other pursuits. And yet, others may have encountered situations that forced them out of sport to pursue success in other parts of their life. I especially enjoyed hearing Dean Cain interviewed on Fox News concerning his superior work ethic. Cain had been an All-American Safety for Princeton University. Upon graduation, he had a promising career in the NFL. However, an injury ended that career and he looked to TV and the movies for his alternative. In his interview, he jokingly remarked about some of the movies he had in order to keep working. Because of his work ethic, Cain always had a job. Regardless of the reason, these athletes attained characteristics from sport that helped them to be successful in other pursuits.

We discussed in the introduction how so many men watch sport and think they could be a professional. According Mullin (2004), a survey of men watching professional sport revealed that fifty-two percent of men believe that they could practice to be professional athletes. Good athletes have a way of making their task appear much easier. They have trained many years to accomplish this task. However, to the untrained eye, it appears much easier. Statistically, if a man played high school football, but did not play during college, he has little chance of playing professionally. Most people have no concept of the hardship of training to be a professional athlete.

A few of years ago, I developed a curriculum and taught a college course, that was used as a pilot study for a national initiative, used by another author, and adapted it for other levels of education (Graham, 2004). In the course, I asked students to interview successful individuals that had been athletes at the college, Olympic, or professional levels. The results included common characteristics that were attained from participation in sport. Some of the common responses included discipline, determination, motivation, commitment and being a part of a team. These types of comments appear in literature written in books by many politicians and other celebrities who came from an athletic background.

Two of my students were the twin sons of a famous body builder from South Carolina. They spoke extensively about their father's accomplishments. Other students had no problem finding former athletes to interview, in the small college town where we lived. One of the local high school coaches was a former track athlete at Duke University and there were more than a few former athletes, including myself, on our college campus.

Students in my course asked former athletes four questions.

1. What sport(s) did you compete in during college?
2. What qualities/characteristics did you acquire from sport that helped you become successful in your chosen career?
3. Did you have aspirations for your current profession when you were in college, or was it something that developed later?
4. What advice would you give a student/athlete based on your experience?

Common responses to question number two included, team work, confidence, discipline, motivation, determination, and commitment. This appears to be repeated in the interviews made by Brian Kilmeade, in his books, "The Games Do Count", and "Its How You Play the Game". For example, Kilmeade is one of the sources that have interviewed Laurie Dhue, a TV reporter, who was also a former Academic All-American swimmer at the University of North Carolina. As the daughter of Bob Dhue, a former executive with the WCW, she would have grown up around sport. Without quoting from his books, I can say that the information derived from Brian Kilmeade's books correlate well to the results of the pilot study that I developed. Although, this material can be found in Wikipedia.org, Celebrina.com, and other sources, Kilmeade is one of the few authors that have written some similar material that may be found in this book. Therefore, every effort has been taken to use other sources for material that may be found in both books.

We indeed, derive characteristics from sport that aid us to be successful in other areas of our lives. Former athletes who chose other careers prove it time and time again. One year a man is a champion wrestler at Princeton, later he is a champion wrestler for the U.S. Navy, and yet, later, Donald Rumsfeld became the Secretary of Defense for the United States. Another athlete was an All-American football player, later he turns down professional football to go to law school. When he begins a successful career in law, World War II begins and the young man joined the navy and becomes a decorated officer. He spent a lifetime of successes in law and politics, and eventually Gerald Ford became President of the United States. And yet, another young athlete methodically planed his music career when he accepted basketball scholarships at colleges and universities near Hollywood so he could become one of the greatest rock singers in history, as Chuck Negron, of Three Dog Night, did. There is a long list of individuals who spent long hours training for sports, and later used the same attributes they developed from sport, in order to excel in other areas of their life.

Motivation is a quality that is difficult to find. Athletes will run wind sprints to exhaustion, practice on weekends and holidays in order to achieve dominance in sports. And different types of sport will teach different attributes to the athlete. While a sprinter learns that explosion into a maximal effort leads to success, the distance runner realizes that speed must be calibrated and measured in relation to the amount of nutrients available to the body over a period of time, in order to maintain a constant effort. An athlete also possesses a unique quality that scientists are only now beginning to realize. During instances of athletic performance, the highly trained athlete seems to have an extraordinary ability to concentrate to the point that the function of the brain changes on demand. Scientists have monitored this activity by using an EEG during athletic performance, illustrating an immediate change to the alpha rhythm of brain activity during times of elevated concentration on athletic performance. Athletes and coaches refer to this as "professional calm", while experts in martial arts refer to it as "Chi". Many other methods of sport psychology have been measured as they apply to the function of the body. If a politician possesses these qualities, the country not only receives a hard working individual that is only concerned with achieving the prescribed goal set forth when they took their oath of office, we also receive an individual that may have an extraordinary gift to focus their minds and bodies on an issue in ways that most people never experience. Likewise, the stage performer is more focused on his/her art, and we observe a greater performance. Entertainers from sports background often compare their craft to that of an athletic performance.

It may not be surprising to discover how many similarities these politicians and entertainers have in common. Whether it is Senator John McCain using the discipline he learned from wrestling and boxing to prepare him to spend years of torture in as a prisoner of war in Viet Nam, followed by his determination to gain a political career after such an ordeal, or Jim Caviezel using the attributes he developed from his basketball training when he had to spend hours hanging from a cross when he portrayed Jesus Christ, in the movie, The Passion of Christ, or pop-musician and former basketball player Chuck Negron comparing his live stage performances to athletics, these athletes shared a common bond.

CHAPTER 2

WHEN ATHLETES RULED THE GOVERNMENT

Many of our country's leaders may have gained positive attributes from competing in athletics that have proven to be assets to them in the administration of our government. Politicians have often been referred to in the media by their athletic background. During recent battles for the presidency, the media often referred to the candidates in this manner. During the most recent presidential race, this issue was raised many times. Mitt Romney had led the 2002 Winter Olympics to success, and had a solid sports background of his own, before running for President, in 2012. During the previous election, John McCain was well known as a former athlete. He was a boxer at Annapolis, and was a reputable wrestler who also played football for Episcopal High School, in Arlington, Virginia. Although, Barack Obama was not a well known athlete, the media aired a televised high school game where Barack "Barry" Obama's name was mentioned.

The Vice Presidential candidates were also memorable athletes. Joe Biden played football, basketball and baseball during high school. Sarah Palin led her high school basketball team to the state championships. However, her college scholarship, when she attended the University of Idaho came from being Miss Congeniality in the Miss Alaska contest. Her husband is a world champion in the Iron Dog Snowmobile race. He has won this 2000 mile race at least four times. President Bill Clinton made reference to Todd Palin completing the race with a broken arm.

Although, his opponents, as well as his own vice presidential running mate have a more significant athletic background, the current hype about President Obama's athletic background is quite interesting. According to a poll aired on Fox News Saturday (Nov. 22, 2008) shortly after he was elected, President Obama was named the second most athletic president. This would be quite a "stretch" considering his predecessors, as well as many congressmen and his own cabinet. It has been well documented on several programs that President Obama was a somewhat average player on his high school basketball team. While this is an admirable accomplishment, many of the U.S. presidents have been college and professional athletes. The hype about the new president was continued when he and his cabinet members were compared to a basketball team. While the analogy was a good one, most of the mentioned cabinet members have a much more impressive athletic background than the President. Around the beginning of the 1970s, Attorney General Eric Holder played freshman basketball for Columbia University. National Security Advisor James L. Jones played forward for Georgetown University's basketball team during the mid-1960s, before joining the Marines. Secretary of Education Arne Duncan was the co-captain for Harvard University's basketball team before playing professional basketball in Australia. The President's personal assistant played basketball for Duke University. According to my friends who teach at NCSU, his first white house press secretary, Robert Gibbs, played goalie for North Carolina State University's soccer team. Of course, his brother-in-law is a college coach and former professional basketball player. This information is not meant to degrade President Obama's athletic background. However, one needs to be cautious when comparing him to other athletes-turned-politicians having a much more impressive athletic record. Most of the recent presidents have a more impressive athletic background than our current one.

Over the years, political campaigns have been filled with similar hype to that of the recent presidential elections. In the 2000 presidential election, Al Gore had played basketball and threw the discus for St. Albans High School, in Washington D.C., while George Bush is quite well known for his background in baseball. President Bush played baseball and rugby at Yale University and was also one of the former owners of the Texas Rangers. Some experts in politics and media have remarked on his profound affect on sport as the President of the United States. Now, there is a new Major League Baseball franchise in Washington.

In the 2004 election, President Bush's opponent was a hockey player from Massachusetts, named John Kerry. The media would often tape Kerry during sport events or passing a football to his running mate, former Congressman and Clemson University wide receiver, John Edwards. President Bush was often shown in the media working out at the gym, running or cycling. Prime Minister Putin of Russia is a former judo athlete who spends a lot of time in the gym, as well. There is also the possibility that Fidel Castro may not have went back to Cuba and become their President if he had a better "drop on his curve ball" when he tried out for a major league baseball team. President Bush has already shown his advocacy for the recent increase in physical education programs. During his administration, physical education had demonstrated a major come-back in our schools, as well as our culture.

As explained earlier, many of our recent presidents have been college or professional athletes. Abraham Lincoln, Teddy Roosevelt, Dwight Eisenhower, John Kennedy, Richard Nixon, Ronald Reagan, and the two presidents from the Bush family were well known for their athletic abilities. However, in recent history, the President that is best known for putting a football in the White House was Gerald Ford. When Ford died at 93, ESPN wrote about his athletic background (ESPN, Dec. 28, 2006). We have discussed much of his life in the introduction of this book. President Ford graduated near the top of his class in high school, where he was the star center for the football team. He played center for Michigan University, one of the elite football programs with the most wins ever recorded, in the NCAA. After achieving All-American status, he refused offers to play professional football for the Green Bay Packers and the Detroit Lions to take a coaching position at Yale University. He coached football and boxing with the intent to enter law school. He actually coached two football players that would later become U.S. Senators (Ohio Senator Robert Taft, Jr. and Wisconsin Senator William Proxmire).

Because of his full-time position as a coach, he was originally denied admission to law school, but eventually was accepted on a trial basis and graduated in the top one third of his class, which included individuals such as former Secretary of State Cyrus Vance and Sergeant Shriver. World War II began shortly after he began to practice law. He joined the Navy where he served as the Athletic Director and Gunnery Officer aboard the Monterey. He illustrated his abilities by winning several battles and being promoted to Lt. Commander in just a few years. Ford's competitive spirit served him in every part of his life. And it would serve him well for the rest of his life as well.

As explained in the introduction, presidents Ford and Reagan were very vocal on how they learned discipline and motivation from competing in football. Ronald Reagan was a President whose athletic background followed him through his career. He began his career as a sportscaster. When he became a major movie star, one of his most memorable roles was in a movie about football. As a politician, his has served as the Governor of California as well as two terms as President of the United States. A college football player, like many of his predecessors, he was also the captain of his college swimming team. Reagan was often ridiculed by other politicians for being over 70 years old during his Presidency. However, he could probably swim faster and longer than most of the younger people who ridiculed him. President Reagan is one of the most memorable politicians in American history. He is thought to be the major contributor for the end of the Cold War. Biographers picture him as a President that stood for honor and integrity in the White House. In a televised biography, it was reported that he would not remove his jacket in the oval office, as a reminder of his sense of honor toward it. He is thought to have been genuinely concerned about the American people, more than he was about himself. These are also characteristics that are required of the captain of a swimming team. One must lead by example on a sports team. It is a quality that served Reagan well as President.

Each member of a team has to be more concerned about the team than the individual, if the team is to have the cohesion required to be successful. Many people outside of sport think that swimmers and track athletes just go out and compete. However, there is a unique strategy in each of these sports. Observers often have no concept of the strategy required for a team to win. For example, one strategy in the 800 meter run is to "box in" the top opponents, behind the best runner on the home team, and to the left of the second best runner on the home team, as they begin the last curve on the track, making it difficult to pass. Being the athlete that "boxes in" opponents, is not a desired position for any track athlete. However, it is part of playing on a team. As a team captain, it is obvious why one must acquire a selfless and enduring attitude. Any leader, especially in sport, is lost, if they are not consistent. Any advocate of coaching education will tell you that consistency is the most important element of a coaching philosophy. Ronald Reagan was a monument to consistency. He was known as a president that united the parties in congress, time and time again, and he never seemed to lose sight of his purpose. Although, he had more to overcome than most presidents, nothing seemed to change his confident attitude. He was shot at, and also recovered from deadly illnesses during his presidency. While the congress was controlled by a political party that was not his own, he negotiated repeatedly with them to accomplish more than most presidents. He was known as "the great communicator".

Another multi-sport college athlete was John Kennedy. As a football player, swimmer and golfer at Harvard University, he shared a common bond with the other two presidents (Reagan and Bush) who cut income taxes during their administration. However, Reagan and Kennedy share a special bond. While they are often referred to as football players, the sport in which they excelled was swimming. Near the end of his life, while Reagan was ill with a disease that causes one to lose some of their memory abilities, it was reported that he could still remember the exact number of people he saved as a lifeguard, during his youth.

President Nixon also played college football for Whittier College in California. However, one of the most memorable, and sometimes controversial athletes to live in the White House, was President Dwight D. Eisenhower. Eisenhower was a football player and a baseball player in college. He was a football star for the West Point football team. However, he also played JV baseball, at West Point with fellow WWII General Omar Bradley. He has been quoted as saying that failing to make the varsity baseball team at West Point was one of the biggest disappointments of his life. However, there has always been a controversy concerning whether Eisenhower had played semi-professional baseball. A Major League baseball player was quoted as saying that Eisenhower had said he played semi-pro ball. This story has been told by numerous radio and newspaper media, and it has been officially, denied by his library, as well as other sources. This controversy may not seem important to most people. However, if he supposedly played semi-pro ball before, playing college football, this would be a violation of NCAA rules. There is also the West Point Honor Code to consider. While Ike graduated in 1915, before the Honor Code of the 1920s was established stating that cadets could not lie, cheat, or steal, it would have been a major problem for someone like President Eisenhower. If the controversy had been true, one might think that President Eisenhower would never talk about baseball. However, he talked about it constantly. He always had a "one liner" about baseball to relate to military tactics, as well at those in politics. He was an avid baseball fan during is presidency. His knowledge of the game would rival President Bush and Senator Zell Miller.

Of course, both members of the Bush family who became president were baseball players at Yale University. George H.W. Bush was a good first baseman in college and when he was president, he could actually "throw heat" when he threw the first pitch at baseball games. Although, George W. Bush is best known as a baseball player, and part owner of the Texas Rangers, he was probably a better rugby player, at Yale. In his 80s, George H. W. Bush was still sky diving and staying in shape. His son George W. is well known for his elaborate workouts, and having a heart rate in the 40s.

Most people do not realize that some of our presidents have been professional athletes. While many people know that Teddy Roosevelt was a professional boxer, he also rowed for the Harvard crew team. Some people know that Abraham Lincoln wrestled. However, few people know that he was actually a professional wrestling champion. Quite a bit of Lincoln's legacy is described in the previous chapter. His appearance often made opponents underestimate Lincoln. They usually found out, the hard way, that looks can be deceiving. However, at 6'4", he would have been a giant in the early part of the 19th century.

These former athletes took the hard work and patience they learned from training for competitive sport and turned it into another admirable discipline. The qualities that made them good athletes served them as good presidents. As explained in the previous chapter, athletics teach us to be patient, enduring, confident, and cooperative with teammates and coaches, as well as good sportsmanship toward opponents. However, the presidency is not the only office where we find athletes in Washington.

Another example of how important athletics is to political competitions could be found in a U.S. Senate race, a few years ago, in Kentucky. Former Congressman Scotty Baesler was running against Senator Jim Bunning for his senate seat. Since Jim Bunning was a former major league baseball player, and Scotty Baesler was a former captain of the University of Kentucky basketball team, the media "played this up" as the baseball player against the basketball player. The baseball player won this tough competition.

In a state where basketball is king, even a major league baseball player like Bunning would have a difficult time against a former UK Wildcat basketball player. It has been said that former Wildcat coach Joe B. Hall doesn't run for governor of Kentucky because it would be a "step down" for his career. When I lived in Lexington Kentucky, I heard Scotty Baesler's name, constantly. He seemed to know everyone. Bunning must have done something special to keep this senate seat.

Not surprising, Bunning has a reputation as a competitor and a hard worker. During his 17-year career as a major league baseball player, primarily as a pitcher for the Detroit Tigers and the Philadelphia Phillies, he accumulated an exceptional record. Retiring from baseball in 1971, he accumulated 1000 strikeouts and 100 wins in both the National League and the American League and currently holds a seat in the Baseball Hall of Fame.

In Kentucky, Bunning also had a record of working his way to the top. He began his political career in 1977, as a member of the City Council, in Fort Thomas, and then becoming a Kentucky State Senator, U.S. Congressman for the 4th District of Kentucky, and then a U.S. Senator. Kentuckians are proud to have this great competitor working on their behalf in the senate.

Another interesting fact relating to Senator Bunning's career is that one of our most recent members of the U.S. Supreme Court is a huge Phillies fan. Judge Samuel Alito was a baseball player, and a little league coach, who has his own "fantasy baseball card" from the Phillies. During his nomination, it was jokingly, reported that, if he was given the choice, he would have chosen to be the Commissioner of Baseball, over being a Supreme Court Justice. During his confirmation hearings in 2006, senators made baseball references when they asked him questions concerning "the highest court in the land".

Nationwide, there are many college and minor league baseball players who served in our Congress. New Mexico Senator Pete Domenici was a pitcher for the Albuquerque Dukes in 1954 (Domenici, 2005). He was thought to be a good pitcher, as well. Georgia Senator Zell Miller is a monument to the importance that sport, more specifically, baseball, plays in our culture. He played for the "old mill" teams that traveled to Georgia, North Carolina and Tennessee, coached at Young Harris College, and used his fame to raise money for baseball programs. He is also famous for catching a foul ball, hit by Deion Sanders, during the 1992 World Series. He was sitting next to former President Jimmy Carter, at the time. Senator Miller is said to be a walking encyclopedia of baseball. In his recent book "A National Party No More" (2003) he used baseball terminology to explain a concept in the 22nd chapter. Senator Miller probably remembers more about Senator Bunning's baseball career than he does.

For many years, there was no shortage of athletes found in Congress. Senator Bunning and Senator Miller were in familiar company in the U.S. Senate. Several of them were at least high school athletes, many of them were college athletes, and a few were professionals like Senator Bunning. Between the college and professional ranks we may have enough football players, in Congress, to field a team. For example, former Seattle Seahawk receiver,

Steve Largent and Canadian Football player J.C. Watts are recently retired Congressmen from the state of Oklahoma. They were each very active members of the House of Representatives, making a reputation for themselves as young congressmen who didn't back down from more established members of Congress, the media, or anyone else that may disagree their political views.

Congressman Largent is well versed in competing at the highest level. As an NFL athlete, Largent was not considered the fastest receiver to ever carry the "pig skin". However, he managed to set the NFL record for receptions before retiring and becoming an Oklahoma congressman. This is by no means meant to degrade any of the fine NFL receivers that may have been faster than Largent. However, it does illustrate how Largent went against the odds to set this record. Drafted out of the University of Tulsa in 1975, he was a record holder in college as well. As a congressman, Largent appeared to be on the "cutting edge" of politics, as he stood for his strong views on moral issues. During a time when morality among politicians had been a major topic for discussion, it was not unusual for many of the older politicians to turn to Congressman Largent for leadership.

J.C. Watts has often been called the "rising star" among young congressmen. He has given the "republican response" after speeches from a democrat president, which seemed unusual for a congressman as young as Watts. He has also been the "popular item" for many political talk shows. Regardless of one's political views, Watts is truly one of the most admirable men in the history of Congress. He always seems to have deep convictions for his views, and unlike many politicians, he does not back down from anyone, regardless of the circumstances. As the only African-American Republican Congressman (during the time he was in Congress), he seemed to get more than his share of ridicule, but it never seemed to sway him. A U.S. Senator who played college football for Harvard and had the opportunity to play professional football for the Green Bay Packers was Edward Kennedy, the youngest brother of President Kennedy (Wikipedia.org, 2013).

Senator William T. Stachowski played football for the College of the Holy Cross in Worcester, Massachusetts. He was elected team captain and received the James Davit Award as a member of the defensive secondary. He was also named as a defensive back on the All-New England Squad in 1971. As an assistant football coach for St. Francis High School, he enhanced the characteristics he acquired as an athlete (Stachowski, 2005).

John Edwards was a good wide receiver and captain of the football team at North Moore High School, and "walked on" the Clemson University team, during the early 1970s, in hopes of winning a scholarship. But he transferred to North Carolina State University (Edwards, 2003). "Walk-ons" understand the importance of practicing the fundamentals of the game to improve their abilities. This concept is very similar in politics. While many more seemingly gifted athletes may not pay as close attention to the fundamentals, a walk-on must be prepared for any opportunity to achieve his place on the team. Likewise, many seasoned politicians may overlook grassroots political programs that serve to overtake their seat.

Other football players in the Congress include former U.S. Senator George Allen, who was an All-ACC quarterback at the University of Virginia (Allen 2005). Senator Allen has an interesting sports background. His father coached for the Rams when they were still in Los Angeles. When he began coaching for the Washington Redskins, George transferred from a major football program in California (UCLA), to the University of Virginia, where he remained. Before becoming a Senator, he was also the Governor of Virginia.

Traveling to the Midwest, we find a three sport athlete at the University of Kansas named Bob Dole. He played football, basketball and ran track, until he volunteered for the military during World War II, where he was severely injured (Dole 2005). Nebraska Senator and Cabinet member, Chuck Hagel, who played for Wayne State University, in Nebraska is another senator that we are beginning to hear much about (Hagel, 2005). Tom Osborne, a Nebraska Congressman, turned down athletic scholarships at major universities, to compete in football, basketball, and track at Hastings College, in his home town, during the late 1950s. He also coached at the University of Nebraska, from 1973 to 1997 (Osborne, 2005). During the late 1960s, Mike Kelly played football for Notre Dame (Kelly, 2011).

Like Watts and Largent, some of the other professional athletes that were former senators include New York Senator Jack Kemp, former quarterback for the Buffalo Bills, and New Jersey Senator Bill Bradley, former forward for the New York Knicks. Both of these men have also been presidential candidates that illustrated the fortitude they had to acquire to become professional athletes before they ever went to Washington. They recently discussed how they had such a great relationship as former professional athletes from different parties in the Senate. A presidential candidate who played football and basketball during college was Kansas Senator Bob Dole. He also ran track for the University of Kansas (Dole, 2005). We have already discussed the competition between presidential candidates and their athletic background. Other presidential candidates will be discussed in following sections.

We have named several senators who were college football players. However, since there are more than four times as many representatives, than senators that make up the U.S. Congress, we should find more football players in this "house" as well. We have named two congressmen from the state of Oklahoma who have been professional football players. However, there are several that played college ball. Shortly, after Senator John Edwards graduated from North Carolina State University (NCSU), Arizona Congressman J. D. Hayworth played football for NCSU. As a 1980 cum laude graduate in communications and political science, in the same mold as President Ronald Reagan, he also worked as a sportscaster in Cincinnati, Ohio, and Greenville, South Carolina (near Edwards' South Carolina hometown), before moving to Phoenix, Arizona, where he served the U. S. Congress from 1994 to 2006 (Hayworth, 2005).

Several other U.S. Congressmen shared the "grid iron" with Hayworth. Tom Allen of Maine, while being a great track athlete played college football, as well. Like Hayworth, he also excelled in the classroom. In fact, he was named a Rhodes Scholar, as well as the National Football Foundation Scholar-Athlete Award, graduating in 1967 from Bowdoin College. He also had leadership positions as the co-captain of his football and track & field teams. Allen stated on his website, that "football taught him, quite forcefully, that good intentions are not enough in this world. We are judged, not by our intentions, but by our performance" (Allen, 2005). This is a lesson that serves Congressman Allen well, as a politician.

Arkansas Senator John Boozman did not travel far from home to play football for the University of Arkansas, during the early 1970s (Boozman, 2005). However, Wisconsin Congressman Ron Kind had to take quite a long trip to play quarterback for Harvard University, and like Hayworth, graduated, with honors, in 1985, from one of the toughest universities in the country (Kind, 2005). John Jack Murtha played "End" for Washington and Jefferson University until he joined the Marines during the Korean War (Murtha, 2005). Like fellow Arizona Congressman J.D. Hayworth, Rick Renzi illustrated his leadership qualities as the captain of the football team at Northern Arizona University when they were in the Big Sky Conference Championships. After graduating in 1980, Renzi remained in the state where he played ball to become one of their congressmen (Renzi, 2005). However, Tim Holden went to the University of Richmond, in Senator George Allen's home state of Virginia, on a football scholarship before becoming a Pennsylvania Congressman (Holden, 2005). The new congressmen, from the 2006 election, include the former quarterback for the Washington Redskins, Heath Shuler, who played college ball for the University of Tennessee, during the early 1990s. He represented western North Carolina until his district was changed in 2012. At some point, Heath would have probably had to play Florida State University, where he could have found one of Pennsylvania's congressmen. Jason Altmire played football for FSU during the same time Heath Shuler was in high school (Altmire, 2009). If he had played one more year, he would have been a senior at FSU when Shuler was a freshman at Tennessee. Ohio Congressman Zackary Space was a Division III All-American at Kenyon College (Space, 2009).

In a recent election, Lynn Swan, the former all-pro receiver for the Pittsburg Steelers ran on the republican ticket for governor of Pennsylvania. If we extend our research to include governors, we would also discover a former college baseball player named Haley Barbour, the governor of Mississippi. We would also have to mention a former professional wrestler, named Jesse Ventura who recently held the position of governor of Minnesota. Of course, we can not speak about governor-athletes without including the multi-time Mr. Olympia, Arnold Swartzeneggar, recently finishing a second term as governor of California.

An interesting story about basketball that refers us back to the U.S. Senate is Senator John Thune. Considered to be the best athlete in the current U.S. Senate, he has reportedly, challenged President Obama to play him in basketball. However, we are not "holding our breath", waiting for this event to take place. Unlike President Obama, Senator Thune was a college basketball player at Biola University, 30 years ago. He is about the same age as the President, but in much better physical condition. Runner's World Magazine (2012) rated Thune as the fastest man in Congress since 2009. At 50, he still ran a 5K in 18:54 in the 2011 ACLI Capital

Challenge. While some of the older congressmen can recall faster times from many years ago, no one in Congress can keep pace with Senator Thune, today. Although, the U.S. Congress has a history of athletes, Senator Thune is one of the few remaining athletes that are still young enough to break 20 minutes in a 5K race. Ten or twenty years ago, Thune would have had his hands full; not only with former college athletes, but with a few former Olympic and professional athletes. However, today the only athletes in Congress young enough to challenge Thune to any sport event would be Ohio Representative Jim Jordan, a two-time NCAA wrestling champion, or Congressman Ron Kind, the former quarterback for Harvard University, and a very few others. This chapter will enlighten readers concerning some of the great athletes who led this country during the 20th century, and a few politicians from the 19th century. The U.S. Congress has been ruled by a long list of college and professional athletes for many years. However, the last professional athlete in Congress recently lost his Congressional district, and most of the remaining college athletes are among the older members of Congress.

Several other basketball players have recently been members of the House of Representatives. A former college basketball player and Rhodes Scholar at the University of Maryland, as well as a professional and Olympic basketball player, named Tom McMillen, was a U.S. congressman for his home state of Maryland. Like Senator Bradley, he also played basketball for the New York Knicks. While Bradley retired from the Knicks shortly after McMillen began his basketball career, they would have been teammates. Like Bradley, McMillen was also an Olympic basketball player. He was actually a member of the 1972 team who has never accepted their silver medal because of the controversy over the 4 seconds placed on the clock that changed the U.S. team's status from the gold medal to the silver medal. Congressman Ander Crenshaw, of Florida, was offered a basketball scholarship to the University of Georgia, where he graduated, in 1967 (Crenshaw, 2005). A couple of years earlier, Bob Etheridge of North Carolina, played for Campbell University, in his home state of North Carolina (Etheridge, 2005). John Tanner, of Tennessee, played for the University of Tennessee, graduating in 1966 (Tanner, 2005). As basketball players, in the same conference, Crenshaw and Tanner would have played basketball against each other. If they could have played as freshmen, Tanner would have played against Congressman Scotty Baesler, who played for the University of Kentucky (Tennessee's rival team) graduating in 1963. Although, Princeton rarely played these universities, they may have played against Senator Bradley during championships and invitations. Congressman Henry Hyde played in the finals of the 1943 NCAA Championships as a member of the Georgetown University basketball team (Hyde, 2013). Indiana Congressman Baron Hill is in the Indiana Basketball Hall of Fame. As a three sport athlete at Seymour High School, in Indiana, he played college basketball for Furman University, in South Carolina (Hill, 2013). New Jersey Congressman Mike Ferguson was a basketball coach at St. Michael Academy (Ferguson, 2005). Another basketball coach was Kentucky Congressman Joe Pitts (Pitts, 2005). Some of the other coaches in the House, include Maryland Congressman Chris Van Holden, who is a veteran MSI Soccer coach (Van Holden, 2005), and Congressman Randy "Duke" Cunningham, who coached swimming at Hindsville High School, where two of his athletes won Olympic medals (Cunningham, 2013).

Two sports we don't hear much from in congress are gymnastics and lacrosse. However, we have some of those, as well. Mary Bono (2005) was a gifted gymnast from California, and Dutch Ruppersberger of Maryland played lacrosse for the University of Maryland, in the Atlantic Coast Conference (ACC), the powerhouse conference for lacrosse (Ruppersberger, 2005). The ACC is where lacrosse meets its major competition, and we find many of its professionals. As the oldest sport in America, it is somewhat strange that we know so little about the sport. However, it is probably the most aggressive team sport in our culture. Similar in practice, to hockey, athletes have to be alert individuals, or they could leave the field with severe injuries. It's like playing hockey without pads.

One of the oldest forms of sport is wrestling. It is well documented in ancient Greek culture. It was also considered the "common man's" sport during the medieval era of Europe. Modern wrestlers are classified in different categories. The commercial form of wrestling is quite different than the wrestling of the ancient Greeks. However, there are two forms of wrestling in the Olympic Games. One is Greco-Roman and the other is free-style wrestling. The form that is most often used in high school and college is free-style. Several anthropometric studies on muscle fiber types have revealed that champion wrestlers tend to have more fast-twitch oxidative muscle fiber than other athletes. This occurrence would be obvious, considering physical abilities that a wrestler must possess. Wrestling is perhaps the only sport where an athlete must compete beyond the "anaerobic threshold". Although, other sports may make this claim, and in some cases, get close to this threshold, wrestling is a sport that requires two athletes, of similar size and strength, to make repetitive powerful movements for two minutes. To the layman, two minutes may not seem like a long time. However, to a power athlete, it is a life time. Unlike other sports where an athlete can recover for a brief time, if the wrestler rests for a moment, he will suffer the consequences of his action. Several congressmen and at least one member of the Bush cabinet were former wrestlers.

A senator that has been in the news quite often during the new century is John McCain. This former Annapolis University boxer and high school wrestler was a POW in Viet Nam for over five years (McCain, 2005). Managing to keep his composure must have been an enormous feat in itself. I am sure that his training as a wrestler helped him in this effort. A wrestler has to acquire a special kind of patience, in order to compete against another athlete of similar physical abilities and wait for an opportunity to act, while maintaining a concentrated effort. I am sure that the combination physical and mental training Senator McCain acquired from wrestling served him well during his years as a POW, and continues to serve him as one of the leaders of our country. Of course, Senator McCain was a college boxer, which will be discussed later. McCain was the 2008 republican candidate for President of the United States.

Across the isle from McCain was a very good college wrestler. The late Senator Paul Wellstone, a democrat from Minnesota, wrestled for the University of North Carolina during the early 1960s (Wellstone, 2013). In ancient Greece, if a tie occurred in a pentathlon, the top two athletes could wrestle to break the tie. If the Senate floor got too heated, maybe the decision could have been settled by a match between McCain and Wellstone. They could actually go to the House of Representatives to get someone to officiate. Not only did the former Speaker of the House, Dennis Hastert, wrestle in college, he also coached for several years. He was a wrestler at Wheaton College, in Illinois, as well as a wrestling coach, and was inducted as an Outstanding American in the National Wrestling Hall of Fame, in Stillwater, Oklahoma, in 2000 (Hastert, 2005). A year later the USOC named him Honorary Vice President of the American Olympic Movement. Dennis Hastert is not someone to be trifled with. He was a steady and cautious leader for the House. During the beginning of the Bush administration, he advised them to execute the new tax cut in increments. This is a choice that would seem obvious to an athlete that was used to controlling his strength for extended periods of time. Speaker Hastert has coached wrestling and knows the importance of waiting for the appropriate time to strike with all of his force. This is a quality that is required for wrestling, and is also good for a politician whose primary function is maintaining order among legislators.

It seems that another former wrestler, like Hastert, was recently our Secretary of Defense. Wrestling seems to run in families. I don't think these two men are related, but they are politicians from the same state and seem to have similar political views. Secretary Donald Rumsfeld wrestled and played football for Princeton and Illinois and then went on to be a wrestling champion for the U.S. Navy. His peers seem to have a deep respect for him and talk as if he is someone who "walks softly and carries a big stick." Many people joke about the pairing of Secretary Rumsfeld with Secretary of State, Colin Powell when they worked together. The common joke was that Secretary Powell could tell the leaders of other countries that they can either negotiate or he will unleash Secretary Rumsfeld on them. Someone once described Secretary Rumsfeld by saying that wrestling is a sport where there is one winner and one loser, and as a champion wrestler, Secretary Rumsfeld had little acquaintance with the concept of losing. Given his well known reputation, he is still a wrestler, at heart. These are the kind of men that Americans always want for their politicians. Wrestlers usually seem to be people that are soft spoken and have that sense of confidence that they don't need to prove they are the "biggest bull in the field." Other wrestlers in the House of Representatives include Ohio Congressman Jim Jordan, a two-time NCAA champion while wrestling for the University of Wisconsin during the mid 1980s (Jordan, 2011). As mentioned earlier, Jordan would be about the only current rival in sport to Senator Thune. Congressman Jim Leach was a 1960 Iowa State Wrestling Champion and a three sport athlete at Princeton (DMU Magazine, 2011). This means he would have wrestled at the same university as Secretary Rumsfeld. He also would have shared a locker room with a basketball player named (Senator) Bill Bradley. He was inducted into the International wrestling hall of Fame in 2009.

A sport that is very similar to wrestling is judo. Colorado Senator Ben Campbell was a gold medalist in the 1963 Pan American Games and the captain of the 1964 U.S. Olympic team. Senator Campbell has a great deal of American pride due to his fascinating background. A Cheyenne Chief, he began his judo experience in the Air Force where he fell in love with the sport. He was a three-time U.S. champion in judo before winning at the Pan American Games and being named captain of the Olympic team. After competing in the Olympics, he went on to coach the Olympic team (Campbell, 2005). Senator Campbell was a passionate athlete and coach. He has also been a spokesman for the rights of Native-Americans. If Senator Campbell had never been a Senator, he would still be an American hero. The sport of judo taught him to be confident and calm in any situation.

As a college judo athlete, the author of this book is well acquainted with the physical and mental demands of judo. Like wrestling, judo is a sport where two opponents of similar size and strength compete beyond their normal physical abilities. One difference to observe concerning judo is there are two completely different ways to win. One way requires an athlete to pin the other submissively for 30 seconds, and the other is to throw the opponent over top of their center of gravity (pelvis), giving them "epon", meaning a full point. This concept requires the competitor to think defensively as well as offensively under extreme conditions. A movement that defends the athlete from an attempt to take him to the mat for a pin may make him vulnerable to a movement leading to "epon". Congressmen often say they are going to do battle "on the floor." However, they should be careful how they use this terminology around former athletes that are used to winning "on the mat.

A U.S. Senate and former Navy (Marine) boxer was James Webb (Webb, 2009). Like fellow boxer and senator, John McCain, he appears to be a patient man who knows when to strike with terminal force. There are so many congressmen and senators that come from the Annapolis boxing team, that when the movie "Annapolis" showed an underclassman being defeated by an upper-class marine, individuals have stated that it could have been based on Senators Webb, McCain or Marine Colonel Oliver North. The boxing match between Senator Webb and Colonel North was quite popular. They were both on the boxing team at Annapolis. Colonel North won that match. While Colonel North was never in the senate, he plays a pivotal role in our country's political environment. This is true of many of our military officers. We also find that many world class athletes came from the military. An entire book could be written on famous military heroes from athletic backgrounds. We have named a few in this book, such as General Patton and Colonel North.

Another one of the oldest sports is track & field. Therefore, we should begin our discussion with the oldest Senator, Strom Thurmond, of South Carolina, who was a distance runner for Clemson University (Thurmond, 2005). We have previously mentioned Maine Congressman Tom Allen, and his many accomplishments in football and academics. He was also co-captain of his track & field team. He was the state champion in the 440 dash, and his relay team set a record for the senior relay. A close neighbor, to the south, is Connecticut Congressman Rob Simmons, who won six varsity letters as he lead the track & field, and cross country teams, as their captain, for Haverford College, in Pennsylvania (Simmons, 2005). As great as these accomplishments are, there is another name that is placed on the board on Capital Hill that is one of the most remembered names in track & field. Kansas Congressman Jim Ryun, the three time Olympian (64, 68, and 72) won the silver medal for the 1500 meter run in the 1968 Olympics, and held the high school record for the mile for 36 years. As a high school and college track athlete, I remember some of the amazing events performed by Ryun. He actually recovered from a terrible fall in one race and still got up and tried to catch the leaders.

Former Kansas Senator Bob Dole is well known for running track at the University of Kansas, an honor he holds with Congressman Ryun. He ran the 440 and the 880, and was quite good at it. However, he also played basketball and football. A severe injury, during World War II ended Senator Doles' exceptional athletic career. Numerous books explain the pain this confident athlete had to endure when he fought to recover from this injury. Winning the Republican nomination in 1996, Dole has been a candidate for President of the United States.

A former U.S. congressman from California is considered the "Worlds Greatest Athlete". Congressman Bob Mathias was a republican, elected to four terms in congress, beginning in 1966. He is the only American who won the Olympic Decathlon, twice. The first time, he was only 17 years old, and when he was asked what he would do to celebrate, he jokingly said he guessed he would start shaving. During college, he was the star half back for Stanford University, during the first televised appearance of the Rose Bowl. Although, he was drafted by one of the professional football teams, he turned it down. During college, he originally turned down the chance to return to the Olympics, and when he finally decided to go, he pulled a muscle in his thigh, during the second event of the decathlon, and won, anyway. He became the spokesman for the 1952 Olympics, made movies, and served in the Marines, before becoming a U.S. congressman. I could write a separate book about this great athlete. Not only have other books been written about him, a movie was made about his life in which he played "himself" in the movie.

Congressmen who compete in sports that are not often mentioned include Nevada Congressman Dean Heller, who is a competitive stockcar racer (Heller, 2009). Congressman Henry Cueller is a third degree black belt in karate (Cueller, 2011). Mary Bono and Peter Roskam were gymnasts (Roskam, 2005). Of course, we can also include congressional candidates such as former New

York Jet Michael Faulkner who ran for the U.S. Congress to re-place Charles Rangel of New York, in 2010. While he did not win, he reflects the many professional athletes in politics.

Other countries are quite proud of their athletes who be-came politicians. In the CBC Sports Online list of the top ten ath-letes who became politicians, nearly half of them are Americans. However, others, such as Dawn Fraser, are from Australia. After becoming the first swimmer to win gold medals in three consecu-tive Olympics, she became a member of the Australian Parliament. Likewise, NHL player, Howie Meeker, became a member of Canadian Parliament (CBC.CA, May 14, 2004).

The U.S. Congress can often be found playing baseball and football games for charities. There are more than enough former college and professional football players to form a team. In the fall of 2007, the Congress played a football game against the Capital Hill Police. Although, the team's coach and quarterback was North Carolina Congressman Heath Shuler, who was also an NFL quarterback, for the Washington Redskins, they lost to the Capital Hill Police. In 1909, the two major congressional parties began playing baseball games. Since 1962, this has been an annual event between the Democrat and Republican parties. During the eight years when NFL All-Pro wide receiver, Steve Largent pitched for the republicans, it was a slaughter for the democrats. During the 2001 baseball game, with Oklahoma Congressman Steve Largent pitching, the republicans won 25 to 1. In fact, the only Democrat who made a run off of Largent noted it on his website. Other congressmen can often be seen in local and national road races. Senator Bill Frist, of Tennessee, has competed in several mara-thons (Frist, 2005). One of the more unique athletes in the senate is Mark Udall, who is quite famous for his mountaineering. He has climbed some of the most impressive peaks in the world (Udall, 2009). We have already discussed Senator John Thune's conquests in local road races, in addition to his background in basketball.

Sport is a microcosm of our society. Therefore, it is represented in the federal government. We can find professional, Olympic and colleges athletes, as well as hundreds of politicians who competed in high school. This book mostly identifies those who were college, professional and Olympic athletes. In the next chapter, we will meet of the pop stars who shared this experience.

CHAPTER 3

ATHLETES ON STAGE

The transition from sport to the stage is a practical one for many reasons. An actor needs to learn about teamwork. Movies are shot in scenes that often do not make sense to individuals outside of the industry. However, the successful actor has to understand that each part of the movie, including scenes that may not pass the final editing process, is all a part of making a movie. This is a crucial, and initially, unsatisfying part of competing on an athletic team. Each team member must realize their role in the game. Otherwise, the coach will have to take them out of the game. This is difficult for fans to understand. But no man can win a game alone. In order to be successful, a coach must consistently shape the athletes into a team. If a wide receiver does not sprint down field when he knows the quarterback is throwing the ball to the tight end, the opposing team will simply team-up on the tight-end. Everyone on the team must play their role regardless of who is getting the glory for it.

Many entertainers have told the story of how they learned discipline from sport. Just as an athlete must consistently practice a skill over and over in order to perfect an athletic performance, Thorndike's Laws of Exercise and Readiness are required for success in the entertainment business, as well. As much as rock stars are ridiculed for some of their lifestyles, their job requires them to rehearse (practice), repeatedly. If an athlete performs a skill five different ways and repeatedly performs one way more than the other four ways, that skill will most likely be the way he/she performs during competition. Therefore, if an athlete trains for an event that requires lots of power and technique, under fatigue conditions, many mistakes will be rehearsed. Therefore, the athlete will be conditioned to compete that way. In the same way, if an athlete only trains under good conditions, he/she will not be prepared for bad ones. This is why a decathlete trains for the hurdles before training for the 1500 meters. During the competition, the hurdles take place during the morning and the 1500 meters takes place in the evening, after the athlete has competed all day (for two days). By the same token, if a musician rehearses in the wrong key more often than in the proper one, the performance will be flawed as well.

An actor also needs to be highly motivated, with a high level of concentration and lots of patience. When they are faced with a problem that ends one part of their career, they must pick themselves up and keep trying to be successful. Losing is often an athlete's greatest experience. They learn what must be accomplished in order to succeed in the event they previously lost. In other situations, when an athletic injury ends an athlete's career in one sport they often find they were really more talented in another sport in which they may not have competed if that injury had not ended their career in their first sport. Actor Kevin Sorbo runs a program for kids called World Fit for Kids, where he teaches them to excel in all of the areas of their lives. He has told the story during interviews of how he called his dad when he was a freshman in college to tell him that his teammates were champion athletes in high school like he was and how that gives you a different perspective on life as an athlete. He further explained about learning from failure to become a champion in all of the areas of your life. A story that will be repeated in this book has to be the one where Kevin Costner visited an acting class being attended by Kevin Sorbo and telling them that they may never make it as an actor. Sorbo came up to Costner at the end of his speech and told him that he would make it in acting. Years later, when they were both playing in a golf tournament, Sorbo reminded Costner that he was in the class that Costner visited that day. Costner replied "you're that guy that told me that you would be a star someday", and further stated "you proved me wrong". Athletes have a characteristic that pushes them to excel when they are told they cannot. Kevin Sorbo maintains that characteristic to excel in all areas of his life, as does Costner. Oddly enough, these two athletes came from very similar backgrounds. They each played high school basketball and baseball and each of them played college baseball and are great amateur golfers today. While it took Costner longer to gain the size to play college basketball, at 6'3", basketball became Sorbo's strongest college sport.

Many athletes have become Olympic champions after an injury knocked them out of another sport. Bruce Jenner was an Olympic champion in the decathlon after being injured in college football. A former water ski champion, Jenner went from college track and football, to a world and Olympic record holder in the decathlon. Today, he is more famous as Kim Kardasian's step father. In contrast, former Congressman Bob Mathias won the Olympic decathlon when he graduated from high school, four years later, he declined to go to the Olympics because he was getting married and wanted to go to medical school. When he decided to compete in the Olympics, one more time, he injured a thigh muscle during his second event and still managed to break the Olympic record in the decathlon. He became the star athlete of the 1952 Olympics. He also turned down a career in professional football. Although, he did get married, anyway, during an interview many years later, he stated that his only regret about going to the Olympics for a second time was that he was involved in so many things after the Olympics, that he never got the chance to attend medical school.

Congressman Mathias' life story is quite the reverse of the situation in our introduction concerning Dr. Archibald Graham. Dr. Graham had left professional baseball and became a doctor. The life of Congressman Mathias helps us to understand what could have happened if Archie "Moonlight" Graham had "got a hit" during his first major league baseball game. He may have stayed in baseball and his hometown would not have had the good doctor that he became.

Many athletes, like Bruce Jenner, find that when one door in sport closes, it opens another door that leads to success. Other athletes, like Congressman Bob Mathias, recognize success in sport, then look for success in other areas, but found it in sport a second time, before going on to find success in other areas of their life. However, many more have recognized their potential in other areas of their life and taken the opportunity to leave sports and excel in another profession.

Another reason many athletes begin careers in the movies is that many action heroes began their career as stuntmen, which requires athletic abilities. While fewer action heroes are former athletes, today, many of the action heroes of the past were required to be athletes, in order to do the stunts that could not be shot in front of a blue screen. For more than one of the previous reasons, a young man who played football for the University of Southern California became one of the biggest stars in the history of Hollywood. Of course, I am talking about John Wayne. He lost his football scholarship when he injured his shoulder in a surfing accident.

The University of Southern California was close to Hollywood. As an athlete, John Wayne was a gifted stuntman with the character to become a great leading man, and for a large man, he also had great agility. This made him a model for other movie cowboys. While teaching sport sociology at a university, I often asked a trick question to my students by asking them "who is the most famous person that played football for USC." Students will go through a list of USC athletes who played in the NFL before I tell them that is incorrect. I did not ask you if they played in the NFL, but who is the most famous among them. The answer is John Wayne.

Reportedly, Wayne influenced Ward Bond, his friend and teammate at USC to become an actor, as well. Wayne and Bond starred in several movies together. Ward Bond played many memorable characters in the movies. Some of them were movies where John Wayne was the leading man, such as the role as a scout in "Hondo", a minister/ranger in "The Searchers", and a priest in "The Quiet Man." However, he played other roles like a track coach in "The Bob Mathias Story", and a union officer in "Gone with the Wind". But he is probably best known for his starring role as the wagon master in the 1950s TV series, Wagon Train.

Several USC football players have become movie stars. For example, Reb Brown, who was not only a football player, but a professional boxer, is probably best known for his role as comic book hero "Captain America" (Brown, 1999). As a tall, muscular, athlete, he was ideal for this character. He actually looked like this comic book hero. He also played in many other roles that required someone to have a great athletic presence, as well as some that did not.

Without naming everyone who played football at USC, there were several other athletes at this university who went on to become major movie and TV stars. One such athlete who left the track team to become a superstar was Michael Landon. As a champion javelin thrower from New Jersey, he went to USC on a track scholarship (Thorpe, 2013). His athletic background is quite well known because of the unusual method he used for sport psychology. He reportedly grew out his hair and the longer his hair grew, the better he seemed to throw the javelin. Like Samson, in the Bible, there seemed to be a relationship between having long hair and throwing the javelin. However, this was the 1950s and most men had very short hair. When his hair was cut, he did not throw the javelin as well, and began a career in the movies, beginning as a teenage werewolf. Afterwards, he became a major TV star as "Little Joe" on the long-running TV series Bonanza. Later, he became the star and director for shows such as "Little House on the Prairie".

During the 1980s, perhaps the most popular TV star was a basketball player from USC, named Tom Selleck. As a college

basketball player, Selleck's athletic abilities were often incorporated into his TV and movie career, especially since he got his first
modeling job because he could "dunk" a basketball with either
hand. Selleck has been interviewed many times concerning his
athletic past. As "Magnum P.I.", Tom often illustrated his athletic ability playing basketball, and volleyball, as well as swimming
and triathlons. He was a gifted senior volleyball player during
the 1980s and was an honorary captain of the Olympic Volleyball
Team, during the 1980s. The show often portrayed Tom's character wearing a Detroit Tigers baseball cap. He was born in Detroit,
and had excelled in baseball, as a teen. Magnum was followed by
a movie called "Mr. Baseball", where Tom was able to demonstrate
his abilities in that sport. In his most recent series, as Jesse Stone,
he played the role of a former professional baseball player who
became a police chief. Because of his many athletic pursuits as an
adult many people think he competed in more than one sport at
USC. However, basketball was his only college sport. The sports
he played as an adult, however, influenced his son, who was an
All-American Volleyball player for a major university in California.
Like fellow USC athlete, John Wayne, Tom was the ideal candidate
for westerns. Today, he is a role model for the western style movies. He has been casted in many westerns that were based on books
written by Louis L'Amour.

A few years after Mr. Selleck graduated from USC, another athlete who would later be portraying a villain in a Louis L'Amour
western with him, was playing quarterback for the rival team of
UCLA. Anyone who doesn't know about his football career must
have been living in a cave. Mark Harmon, the son of 1940 Heisman
Trophy winner and professional football player and coach, Tom
Harmon, was destined for a career in the NLF. However, Mark
chose to be an actor. Like Selleck, he has one of the most impressive resumes in Hollywood. While most movie stars from a professional sports background only left after an injury or some other

major incident beyond their control, caused them to leave, Mark did the opposite. Rather than continue a career in professional football, like his father, he chose Hollywood. Graduating cum laude from UCLA, it is not surprising that Mr. Harmon became a successful actor. Today, Mark is the star of the popular TV series, NCIS.

Football was such a dominant force in the Harmon family, that when Mark's sister became a TV star on the Ozzie and Harriet Show (according to a movie about the Nelsons), after she married their son, Ricky Nelson, she made the comment that she was finally getting some fame, after growing up in a family where everyone was a famous athlete. However, her new father-in-law, Ozzie Nelson, had also been a notable college football player at Rutgers University.

If Mark Harmon had attended UCLA 15 or 20 years earlier, he would have shared a locker room with one of the many athletes to play in Tarzan movies. During the 1950s, Denny Miller played basketball for UCLA (briansdriveintheater.com, 1999). There are many references concerning this former basketball star. Many of them illustrate someone that holds a special value to this book. As a large muscular athlete, it seems that Denny was "discovered" by an agent while working his way through grad school, moving furniture. In a TV program about actors who played Tarzan, Denny jokingly, explained how he was in his early 20s and went out and did whatever stunt the directors thought Tarzan should do. After playing the role of Tarzan, Mr. Miller co-starred in the TV series "Wagon Train", the TV show that formerly starred Ward Bond. He later played in many other roles such as a Tarzan-type role in "Gilligan's Island". He was another actor that had a unique athletic presence that resonated with the public. Denny was one of those actors who we saw in many movies. Some of them were movies in which he was a character actor. He is also well known as the model for a popular TV commercial. He actually published a book about how people recognized him without remembering his name, entitled, "Didn't You Used to be What's His Name". This concept in his book is a key part of this book and we will discuss Denny again, later in this chapter. Many of the athletes named in this book would fit well in Miller's book. In fact, another UCLA athlete that probably shared the locker room with Miller would have been a football player named Brad Harris, who later played in a lot of "sword and sandal" movies (briansdrivintheater.com, 1999). Brad was another athletic actor who played in many roles where someone would wonder about his athletic background. Did you ever wonder who the big guy was in James Bond's, "Diamonds Are Forever"? That was professional wrestler and body builder, Joe Robinson (briansdriveintheater.com, 1999). Many of these athletes-turned-actors will be discussed in this book.

Los Angeles is a big city, and universities like USC and UCLA are not the only schools. Since Hollywood is in Los Angeles, another basketball player chose California State University at Los Angeles from his many scholarship choices. A couple of years before the time Tom Selleck was playing basketball for USC, one of the biggest stars of rock & roll began planning his career through his abilities in basketball. As a 6'5" talented athlete, Chuck Negron had numerous basketball scholarship offers. He methodically, chose universities in southern California, finishing at CSULA. He already had a band when he finished college. Shortly afterwards, he began the band we all remember as "Three Dog Night". Selling millions of records, it became one of the top bands of all time (Chucknegron.com, 2013).

While we are discussing athletes from universities in California, we must refer back to the introduction of this book to discuss a baseball player from the CSU at Fullerton, named Kevin Costner. As discussed earlier, Mr. Costner was an exceptional college athlete. According to one of his classmates, he was also a good basketball player in high school. This is often revealed in his many movies about sports. It is very difficult for the best actors to portray "athletic grace" if they were never athletes, themselves. As a gifted athlete, Kevin did this feat very well. Some of his movies about baseball include For the Love of the Game, Bull Durham, and Field of Dreams.

While we are referring to the athletes discussed in the introduction, we could list many of the actors in the movie "Field of Dreams" that were former as well as current athletes. For example, Timothy Busfield, who has been in more than one movie about baseball, played semi-pro baseball (Busfield, 2013). However, perhaps the best casting in the movie was Burt Lancaster. Only a great athlete that had chosen a different path in life could have played that role with such passion and authenticity. Burt Lancaster was an incredible athlete. We have all heard Robert Osborne (Turner Classic Movies) discuss Burt Lancaster's athletic background and how he portrayed his abilities in movies. As a younger actor, he played in movies such as The Crimson Pirate where he performed amazing stunts and made then look easy. He was such a great athlete that he was chosen to play the role of Jim Thorpe in the biographical movie about Thorpe. Burt played this role during a time when there was no "trick photography" that could make someone appear to be athletic. This role could only be played by another great athlete.

When we try to determine the best athletes in Hollywood, several names come to mind. These are usually someone that has recently left professional or Olympic sports to become an actor. However, the people who have been in this business for a long time might give other names. This book, mostly, concerns personalities who were former athletes and became successful in areas other than sports, which made them successful athletes, and entertainers because they derived some special qualities from participation in those sports. These personalities are more difficult to identify since their fame is not based on their athletic performance.

We have explained some of the great athletic achievements of Burt Lancaster. He was considered one of the greatest athletes in the history of Hollywood. We also mentioned an actor who often played in movies with Burt. This great wrestler was Kirk Douglas. Lancaster and Douglas each performed stunts in the movies that have been copied time and time again by stuntmen in more recent movies. Some of these were "signature stunts" that each of them performed as much older actors. One must also remember Lancaster's partner in the circus, Nick Cravat, who played with Lancaster in several movies, especially the action movies such as The Crimson Pirate. As we will find in this book, great athletes often play well-known monster roles in the movie. Cravat is quite well known for an episode of The Twilight Zone, where he played the role of a "gremlin", on the wing of a plane.

Another circus performer-turned-stuntman, and then as one of the most memorable TV characters in history, was Clayton Moore, "The Lone Ranger". As an acrobat and a "catcher" on the trapeze, Moore was exceptionally strong, and began his career as a stuntman. In an interview with some of the movies stars that played with him during his early years, Gene Autry recalled that he reportedly put other stuntmen in the hospital when he would accidentally hit someone in a "fighting scene". One of these actors explained that Clayton was also "fearless", and performed many stunts for the first time as if he had practiced them for years. Like Douglas and Lancaster, he was still performing many of these stunts as an older actor.

When discussing actors that came from a more traditional form of athletics, we may recall famous actors from professional baseball, football or basketball. However, few of them played more than one professional sport. However, before Bo Jackson became famous for being a professional athlete in two sports, another athlete accomplished this feat, but then became more famous as an actor. Chuck Connors, "The Rifleman," played basketball for the

Celtics before playing baseball for the Cubs and the Dodgers. He has some of the best stories about athletes becoming actors. First, he was remembered as the first professional basketball player to break a backboard. However, he also tells one of the funniest stories in the history of television and the movies, when he describes how he became an actor.

It seems that while he was playing baseball in a game in Los Angeles, he was getting a little bored. After seeing a "bull fight," and watching how that the matador is paraded around the ring for 20 minutes after he wins the bull fight, he thought that he might try something similar after his next home run on the baseball field. So the next time he hit a home run, instead of running the bases, he turned to the umpire and asked him if he saw how he hit that ball. Of course, the umpire told him, in a very intimidating way to get his "butt" around those bases. But Chuck had another idea. He said there is no rule that says that he has to run the bases, so he did a sort of fancy walk to first base. Then he did a" slide" at second base, then did "cart wheels" to third base. The third base coach remarked "what are you doing" and Chuck simply replied, using another form of light humor. Then he ran to home plate and jumped up on the fence and acted like a monkey. An agent was watching the baseball game and said that he needed to talk to this guy about a career in the movies and television.

Americans are very fortunate that this agent made that decision. As one of the children that grew up in the 60s and 70s, I remember getting a toy "Rifleman Rifle" for Christmas. I'm sure many of the readers of this book have the same memory. Chuck Connors has been one of the best role models for children growing up in the 60s and 70s, with roles like "The Rifleman", "Branded", and "Cowboy in Africa". Many times, Connors demonstrated the importance of using athletes in action-westerns. Like his predecessors, Mr. Connors did stunts on these shows that are still copied by stuntmen in today's westerns. Connors was one of the few actors that demonstrated that "athletic grace" that is not easily copied. He was quite well known for the way he could leap on a horse.

Other baseball players in the entertainment business include actors, Kurt Russell, Bing Russell, Drake Hogestyn, Robert Redford, George Clooney, Tom Selleck, and Billy Crystal, as well as musicians such as Tim McGraw, Billy Ray Cyrus, Charlie Pride and Roy Acuff. Charlie Pride played minor league baseball, while Roy Acuff played semi-pro ball. While we could probably write a book on all of the entertainers who played high school ball, these athletes played college or professional ball. In some cases, athletes have turned down the chance to play college or professional baseball, in order to pursue another career. George Clooney tried out for the Cincinnati Reds during high school. When he did not make the team, he attended Northern Kentucky University. I don't recall him having a baseball scholarship at NKU, before moving to California to become a movie star. David Hartman, actor-tuned-talk show host on Good Morning America, turned down offers to play professional baseball, as well as college baseball, in order to get an Economics degree from Duke University (Wikipedia. org, 2009). Before anchoring Good Morning America, he also co-starred in TV series' such as The Virginian.

Tim McGraw is quite well known as a baseball player. He not only played baseball for Northeast Louisiana State University, he was also the son of the All-Star Major League Baseball player, Tug McGraw. Kevin Costner is not the only former college baseball player to play the game in the movies. Although, Robert Redford has starred in many different movies, he was well equipped to star in "The Natural". He had been a college baseball player for the University of Colorado (Wikipedia, 2005). Another example for this occasion could be found in one episode of the top TV soap opera, "Days of Our Lives". Drake Hogestyn's character was explaining why a Yankee fan could not have a room in his house painted "Philadelphia Phillies Red". Drake Hogestyn (Wikipedia, 2013) had been a professional baseball player for the Yankees organization until he became an actor. He is another actor who has been asked many times, in many forms of media, about his baseball career. Once he started acting on the very popular soap opera, Days of Our Lives, his character progressively, became the star of the show. Talk show hosts have asked him how someone goes from a Pre-Dentistry student at the University of South Florida to professional baseball, and then day time TV. Reportedly, Drake was looking for something to do during the 'off season", when his "off season" job became his career.

As a native of Kentucky, I remember Billy Ray Cyrus and George Clooney. While I did not know George, personally, everyone knew he came from a family of entertainers and politicians. We all know his aunt Rosemary from the movie White Christmas. We also knew that George was a good baseball player at a high school in northern Kentucky. On the other hand, Billy Ray Cyrus and I had several mutual friends. He was the son of Ron Cyrus, one of our state legislators, in eastern Kentucky. Billy received a baseball scholarship at Georgetown College, in northern Kentucky, about 50 miles south of Northern Kentucky University, where Clooney was going to college. Billy was a very good baseball player that I thought would go pro after college. Graduating from East Carter County High School, in Grayson Kentucky, I ran track against Billy's high school, and had some good friends, there. However, I was a little older than Billy, and I vaguely knew him. However, one of his band members graduated from East Carter, and was a close friend to my brother, John. Although, George and Billy were about the same age, and grew up fairly close to each other, I do not know if they ever played ball against each other, unless it would have been during a championship tournament. However, since each of their families included Kentucky politicians, I suspect, their parents knew each other.

Perhaps one story about baseball players becoming actors that could rival the story about Chuck Connors is the one about Kurt Russell. This was a guy that had been a child actor, and then a professional baseball player until an injury caused him to look elsewhere for employment. He has been quite candid during interviews, such as First Person with Maria Shriver, relating how he only became a movie star after his injury knocked him out of professional baseball. However, an interesting twist to this story is that Kurt's father, Bing Russell, had played minor league baseball (Labrocque, 2014, Jan 13). Bing also became a movie and TV star in roles such as the sheriff on the TV series, "Bonanza". Although, Bing was an actor at the time his son was choosing baseball over acting, he coached his son to be a great baseball player. Like his father, Kurt only considered a career in the movies after his injury.

While Billy Crystal (2013) was a very good baseball player at Marshall University, we have seen more of his baseball expertise, off-screen, as a middle-aged man. In fact, several of these ball players have played in numerous exhibition and charity games. Kevin Costner and Billy Crystal have often been seen in these games. Michael Bolton and Garth Brooks are well known for playing a series of games while on the road with their respective bands. One of the newest baseball players to begin his acting and modeling career after an injury ended his professional baseball career with the Tampa Bay Rays is Anderson Davis (Andersondavis.com). His Kraft Zesty Salad Dressing commercial has been quite popular.

It is difficult to isolate some of these athletes by sport. As we explained on the previous pages, Chuck Connors had not only played professional baseball, but also professional basketball. While such a feat is rare in professional sport, many of these athletes have played more than one sport in college. Unlike today, when children grow up only playing one or two sports, during previous generations, good athletes excelled in multiple sports. Later in this chapter, we will discuss a movie star who "lettered" in eight sports during college.

Another athlete that is well known for his many athletic abilities is Dr. Bill Cosby. In 1984, he was inducted into the Temple University Hall of Fame (Cosby, 2007). According to the Temple Athletics website, Bill played full back on the football, as well as basketball. However, he excelled in track and field. He ran the hurdles, threw shot, discus and javelin, and was the MAC high jump champion in 1962. One might wonder why he did not compete in the decathlon. While competing in all of these sports for the Navy, specifically the Quantico Marines track team, he may have competed against a Marine officer named Bob Mathias, who would have still been in the Marines, in 1956, when Bill joined the military. Some of his early comedy routines were about running track for Quantico. As a young track athlete, I remember listening to his recordings, repeatedly. It was obvious that he had experienced all of the funny aspects about running track. Anyone who has ran the 400 meters, knew what Bill Cosby meant when he said "the bear met him on the second turn and gave him a stove and refrigerator and told him to carry it the rest of the way".

After watching Garth Brooks play baseball, during his country music tours, one has to wonder how he had time to play baseball in school, since his athletic scholarship came from throwing the javelin on the track team, at Oklahoma State University (Wikipedia. org, 2013). Baseball and track are during the same season. It is difficult to schedule time to play the many baseball games in a season, while running track. Jock Mahoney (Tarzan) competed in football, basketball, and swimming (briansdriveintheater.com). Swimming normally overlaps basketball season. This is a difficult schedule to manage. However, many athletes have managed it. According to IMDB.com (2007) and several other websites, Kevin Sorbo was a four-sport athlete at Moorehead State University, in Minnesota (currently Minnesota State University at Moorehead).

He played football, hockey, baseball, and basketball. While football, basketball, and baseball cover all of the seasons in college sports, playing center, on the hockey team, overlapped his other sport schedules, most importantly basketball, which was the sport in which he is best known.

As a college athlete, at Morehead State University, in Kentucky, I often heard about "the other Morehead State University", spelled Moorehead State. Although, we never competed against each other, after I graduated, I had a friend who knew Kevin, well, and often bragged about him. Interestingly, the quarterback for our football team at Morehead was Phil Simms, the former Super Bowl MVP, and All-Pro quarterback for the New York Giants. Phil is currently, nationally known as a sportscaster and has played in some movies. Although, I do not recall Morehead State University ever playing against Moorehead State University, Kevin and Phil are each great athletes, who have a lot in common, and are very admirable men, who played college football around the same time, at universities with similar names.

One of the sports in which Kevin Sorbo and Tom Selleck each excelled, was basketball. As mentioned earlier, Tom Selleck is still best known for his TV role as Thomas Magnum, in Magnum P.I., which was an icon of the 1980s, and still syndicated to this day. We can often see Tom playing basketball on this show, as well. As stated about some of the baseball players in this book, actors from a basketball background are often asked to demonstrate their abilities on TV and in the movies as well. Tom Selleck is well known for being introduced to modeling when someone was needed that could "dunk" a basketball with either hand. Likewise, Kevin Sorbo, played college basketball at Moorehead State University, in Minnesota, and demonstrated his athletic abilities on the silver screen. Apparently, Kevin was quite good. I recently spoke to a student at MSU, who described the section, in their trophy case, devoted to Kevin Sorbo.

Like Selleck, Kevin also began his career as a model, and starred in movies and TV, but is also best known for his TV role as "Hercules", an icon of the 1990s that became the top TV show in the world, and is also a very popular syndicated show, very much like Magnum P.I., starring Tom Selleck. While it might not be appropriate for Hercules to play basketball, the game Kevin loved so well, was incorporated in Andromeda, the series in which he starred for the following five years. In more than one interview, Kevin explains a theme of this book, very well, when he described how he decided, during college, that he would not become a professional athlete.

Some of the other college basketball players on the silver screen include Denny Miller, Jim Caviesel, Ted Cassidy, Marc Blucas, Mike Connors, Jock Mahoney, and Bob Barker. Denny Miller first became famous as Tarzan. Miller was an enthusiastic character, as Tarzan. When he was asked to do a stunt that would frighten most of us, he just went and did it. And Miller still has fun with it. During an interview of actors who played the role of Tarzan, he stated that he warned children that if he did his Tarzan yell for them, animals would stampede. Miller went on to play in other TV shows such as "Wagon Train", and mini-series' such as "V". Like Kevin Sorbo, Denny Miller has lived a life that is crucial to the theme in this book. We will talk about him again in this chapter.

Who can forget the TV game show icon, Bob Barker? Several years ago, I taught in southwestern Missouri, near Drury College, where Bob went to college on a basketball scholarship until WWII took him elsewhere. Like basketball players Chuck Connors, Senator Bob Dole, Jock Mahoney and many other athletes of their generation, World War II changed everyone's plans. We will continue to discuss the events that took place in the lives of these athletes that changed the direction of their careers from sport to entertainment.

One of the younger movie stars who played well enough to be offered basketball scholarships to college was Jim Caviezel.

Having played basketball for Bellevue Community College, Jim is well known for many roles, after a foot injury ended his basketball career (IMDb.com, 2013). However, he is best known for perhaps the most difficult role ever played. He played Jesus Christ, in the movie, The Passion of Christ. This role was extremely physically demanding. To make crucifixion look as real as Jim did, without killing oneself, is a hard act to follow. Jim recently began starring in the popular TV series Person of Interest. However, like many of the other athletes we have discussed, one of his first roles was as a basketball player in a movie about college basketball called Blue Chips.

Another young (near 40) actor who played college basketball was Marc Blucas, a former basketball player at Wake Forest University, who played pro ball for the Manchester Giants, in England (IMDb.com, 2013). The son of two educators, Blucas also excelled academically, winning the Murray Greason Athletic Academic Award. Destined for law school, Blucas decided to become an actor, taking major roles such as the starring roles as athletes in Pleasantville, Summer Catch, and Touchback and most recently a starry role in Necessary Roughness, a TV show about sports agents.

Anyone who has watched the syndicated 1960s comedy, "The Adams Family" had to wonder if the guy playing Lurch was a basketball player. Of course, Ted Cassidy played basketball for Stetson University, in Deland, Florida (Wikipedia.org, 2013). Ted continued in many action movies, as well as other comedy roles, such as he did in one episode of "The Beverly Hillbillies", where he bended Granny's shotgun. Basketball was one of Jock Mahoney's many college sports. However, he is discussed, extensively, later in this chapter.

A newcomer to TV and the movies is former NBA basketball player, Rick Fox, who played college ball at UNC, during the same time that Academic All-American Laurie Dhue was a swimmer there. Laurie, of course, became a Fox News Anchor. Rick played pro ball for the Celtics and the Lakers before becoming an actor.

Rick Fox is not the only NBA player to star in movies. Marques Johnson, at 6'7" played from 1977 through 1990 in the NBA with teams such as the Bucks, Warriors and the Clippers. He has been in several movies. We can't forget our basketball players turned actors over 7 feet tall. Kareem Abdul Jabar (Airplane) and Wilt Chamberlain (Conan The Destroyer) have played in many movies. Of course, we cannot forget Dr. Shaquille O'Neal, the 7'1" center for The Heat who has held several starring roles unrelated to basketball as well as playing in movies related to basketball with Johnson and Fox, as well as Blue Chips with Jim Caviezel. As one of LSU's newest PhDs, O'Neal keeps building his resume.

Several musicians have also "aimed for the peach basket". Country artist Billy Dean went to college on a basketball scholarship, as did rock artist Chuck Negron, of Three Dog Night, who played college basketball for California State University at Los Angeles, and Allan Hancock College, in Santa Maria, CA. His online biography explained that moving from New York to Santa Maria, followed by the move to Los Angeles made it possible for him to get closer to the music business while playing college basketball. He compared live music performances to an athletic event (chucknegron.com). Country music artist, Billy Dean, played basketball for East Mississippi Community College (Wikipedia.org, 2013). Oddly enough, Negron and Dean have both played in Dean's hometown of Nashville, Tennessee. As a current resident of Nashville, some of my friends, have claimed they have played basketball with both of them at Belmont University, where country music star (and one of the best golfers in entertainment) Vince Gill produced a celebrity basketball tournament which stars athletes like Dean and Negron. Tom Chapin is another basketball player, who played in a pop band with his brother Harry Chapin, and also hosted his own TV show, called "Make a Wish" (Wikipedia.org, 2013).

Many professional wrestlers have become actors. But before they were wrestlers, many of them were basketball players. All we need to do is read some of the college basketball rosters to find some of these tall athletes. At 6'10", Mark Callaway began his athletic career playing basketball for Angelina College, in Lufkin, Texas, then spending several years as "The Undertaker" in professional wrestling. Today, while he is still a professional wrestler, he also plays roles in movies. Kevin Nash, another 6'10" professional wrestler, not only played college basketball for the University of Tennessee, he played professional basketball in Europe, before becoming a champion wrestler. He has contributed to a list of movies that include DOA, and The Punisher. One of the all-time largest wrestlers was former Wichita State University basketball player Paul "Big Show" Wight. At well over 7 feet tall and nearly 500 pounds, he is the likeness of Andrea the Giant, who also starred in many movies such as The Princess Bride. Paul has also been in many movies such as Knucklehead and Waterboy.

We have discussed Mark Harmon, one of the best quarterbacks in the history of UCLA football. Playing football is a very good preparation for acting. Both of these professions require a man to remember how to execute several applications, and to make quick decisions if a situation changes. If a wider receiver does not know how to interpret the play called by the quarterback, he can not be in the right place, at the right time, to catch the ball. It is no wonder that the leading man in one of this generation's top television series played wide receiver for Columbia University. His name is Matthew Fox. Before becoming one of the stars in TV's "Lost", this rancher from Wyoming, had other starring roles in "Party of Five", as well as movies that required him to illustrate his physical and mental gifts when asked to play roles that are very physically demanding or require an athletic character. He recently starred as Racer X, in the live-action adaptation of the animated series called "Speed Racer" (TV Guide, 2007, December 31). In the movie "We are Marshall", he played a football coach. While watching the movie, I remember thinking, "this man has played some football". In one scene he had to explain a football "play" to one of the young receivers. His ability to explain the fundamentals of the "play" sounded more like a real coach, than an actor playing the role of one. It was obvious that Mr. Fox knew more about football than what an actor would learn in preparation for a movie. Matthew Fox is a gifted athlete that appears to know his way around a football field. In an interview with Sports Illustrated (2006, November 30), he said he was not the fastest man on the field, and compared himself to a famous NFL wide receiver, who was the type of athlete that always got back up after running the pattern and being clobbered by the defense. While he did not compare himself to Congressman Steve Largent, this was the talent that made Largent an All-Pro, receiver for the Seattle Seahawks. During the interview, he was also asked about the win against Princeton that ended Columbia's 44-game losing streak. A year earlier, the free safety that would have been "clobbering" Fox, would be Dean Cain. Cain was the star free safety for Princeton University who had graduated the year before this game, and signed with the Buffalo Bills. However, a knee injury ended his professional football career before the first game. However, like Fox, Cain became a TV and movie star shortly after graduation. He is probably best known for his role as Superman, in the TV series, "Lois and Clark". Cain was also a great volleyball player at Princeton. In an episode of Off-Camera with Dean Cain, Matthew Fox took Dean Cain Fly-Fishing. During the show, Dean Cain aired a film of the two of them playing football against each other when Princeton played Columbia. In the clip, Fox was catching a high pass from his quarterback and ran out of bounds, while All-American Safety Dean Cain was running toward him as he ran out of bounds.

If Matthew Fox had played for Columbia University, nearly twenty years earlier, actor Ed Harris (The Abyss, The Rock, and The

Right Stuff) would have been one of his teammates (Wikipedia. org, 2009). When Ed Harris began playing for Columbia, another football player began playing quarterback for the Pittsburg Steelers. Co-starring in several movies, Terry Bradshaw (Failure to Launch), is considered one of the greatest quarterbacks in the history of the NFL. However, he was probably most famous as a javelin thrower during college, and probably would have placed well in the 1972 Olympics, if he had not became a professional athlete in 1969. Duck Dynasty's Phil Robertson was actually the starting quarterback at LTU during that time.

Another football player-turned-entertainer has something in common with Mr. Bradshaw. After playing college ball for Ohio University and Youngstown State University, Ed O'Neill went to training camp in Pittsburg, in 1969 with Terry Bradshaw. After not making the final cut for the Steelers, he returned to the Youngstown area to teach high school before becoming a household name as "Al Bundy" in the popular TV show "Married with Children". On the show, his character repeatedly made references to playing high school football. One of the common scenes was when he reminisced about throwing four touch-down passes in a single game in high school. While the role was supposed to be comical, the actor was a very good college football player who was really considered by professional teams. Mr. O'Neill has often played coaches in the movies (TV.com, 2008). Like Matthew Fox, he seems to have a unique "presence" when playing coaching roles.

A wide receiver, originally drafted by the Buffalo Bills, in 1976, played ball during the time Bradshaw was starring on the grid iron. Forry Smith is one of the hardest working actors in Hollywood and usually appears in roles where an athletic appearance in needed, such as his starring role as Reece Walker, on the soap opera, Santa Barbara. At 6'3" and very athletic, he was ideal for a role that required the star to be an athlete, such as the ex-boxer role he played in Santa Barbara. After an injury in 1977, ended his football career he was an English teacher before becoming a movie star and finally using his teaching talents to become a screen-writer for movies such as Paparazzi, a movie is which he also had a small role as a police officer. Smith is one of those guys that you see on TV or in a movie and think "wasn't that guy at professional athlete"?

Another professional football player who received roles where an athletic appearance was needed was Jeff Severson. A former safety for the Redskins, Oilers, Broncos, and Cardinals, during the 1970s, Severson also coached at Long Beach State University during the early 1990s. Severson was one of those actors that you would see in a movie about sports and say "I've seen him in other sports movies, but don't know who he is". He actually looks a lot like Forry Smith. While he was well-known in the movie "The Best of Times", as the quarterback for the opposing team, his name is not in the credits in other movies where I recognized him. Jeff, like Forry Smith, is one of those "athletic looking" actors that you see in a lot of movies even when they are not in the credits. They would have each been someone that would fit well in Denny Miller's book, "Didn't you use to be What's His Name". All three of these men are tall, athletic, blonde-headed men who were often asked to play in these character roles. However, the NFL football player who might rival Denny Miller for playing these types of roles is the former NFL football player Tim Rossovich. During his time as an All-American at USC, he was Tom Selleck's roommate. With a body size similar to that of Denny Miller, he has played in many character roles as athletes and other action characters. When he played in a few episodes of Magnum P.I. with his college roommate, with his dark hair and mustache, he was referred to as a more beefy looking version of Tom Selleck. We have all seen these guys in movies. They are the ones you watch in action roles and movies about sport and then try to look them up in some sports magazine to see where they played ball. As referred to earlier in this chapter, this concept is a major component of this book. Whether it was a Tarzan movie or a movie about sport, we always need to have these guys to make the movie appear legitimate. Later, we will discuss Charles Starrett, who played football for Dartmouth. According to Briansdriveintheater.com (2012), his first movie was The Quarterback, which was partially filmed at Dartmouth a few years after he graduated.

Another relationship with Terry Bradshaw can be found on country music stages all over the world. At 6'6" and roughly, 250 pounds, Trace Adkins is one of those musicians who possess a unique "athletic presence." He played defensive end on the football team at Louisiana Tech University (Gardiner, 2012, Feb). Adkins still works out as if he was still playing ball. While I live near Nashville, I have never met him. However, I know a lot of his friends who always say good things about him. Everyone I know who has met him for the first time always tells me that he treats strangers like old friends. If he had not been injured, maybe he would have played semi-professional football against Toby Keith, who has went on tour with him, and who played football for the Oklahoma City Drillers. As a defensive end, he would have lined up across from the tight end, the position played by Toby Keith. Toby is one of the few musicians similar in size to that of Adkins. On Fox News Sunday (August 3, 2008), Toby jokingly said that he was too big to play linebacker and too slow to play any other position. It makes you appreciate athletes who play at that level. He said that he makes his living writing songs. Another country music star named Gary Morris, played football for Cisco Junior College. When I was a graduate student at Middle Tennessee State University, I recall that Morris' son was one of the best high school athletes in Tennessee. Kris Kristofferson was a football player and Golden Gloves boxer during college at Pomona College in California before he was a singer-songwriter and actor (Wikipedia.com, 2013). He also played in the movie Semi-Tough with fellow football player, Burt Reynolds.

One of the many pro football players who found a successful career in entertainment after an injury ended his football career is country music star, Mike Reid. An All-American at Penn State and Heavyweight Wrestler during the late 1960s, Reid was a defensive lineman for the Cincinnati Bengals from 1970 to 1974. A few years ago we lost a football player-turned-musician. Clarence Clemons played football for the University of Maryland, Eastern Shores. Although, an injury ended his football career after trying out for the Dallas Cowboys and Cleveland Browns, he played in the 2009 Super Bowl, playing sax for the East Street Band (New York Times, June 2011).

One of the most memorable western stars was Randolph Scott. He originally went to college playing football at Georgia Tech University. The university's web-site still portrays a photo of Scott. After an injury ended his football career, he moved to Charlotte, North Carolina to finish his degree in textile engineering at the University of North Carolina before becoming a major movie star. Although, he had served in WWI, his football injury kept from becoming a Marine in WWII. Like Arnold Schwarzenegger, Scott invested the money he made from the movies, and became quite wealthy. Both of these men are quite well known for using the money they made in movies in order to invest it elsewhere, becoming much wealthier than their peers.

Another unique relationship that should be made, concerning Randolph Scott, is that he was close friends with perhaps the most remembered man of the 20th century. As a native of North Carolina, before becoming a movie star, he lived near Charlotte, and the Rev. Billy Graham's family owned a dairy farm nearby, and as a teenager, Billy often had to deliver the milk. Randolph Scott was one of his customers. Later, these two men would become close friends and golf partners (Graham, 1999). Billy Graham also preached at his friend's funeral.

Other football players that made their way to the silver screen included Dan Blocker, a former Sul Ross State University football player that we all remember as "Hoss Cartwright" on the TV show "Bonanza". Playing football for a university in west Texas, made playing in westerns a good role for Dan. At 6'3" and a solid weight near 300 pounds, one would assume that he played football (Blocker, 2013). However, Dan was not alone on this TV show. David Canary, who played the role of "Candy", the foreman for the Ponderosa, played football for the University of Cincinnati. During an interview (2008, emmyTVLegends.org), he explained that when he was drafted by the Denver Broncos, he turned it down. When he was asked why, he jokingly, replied that when he graduated from UC, he only weighed 172 pounds and he would have been killed in professional football. He is now a soap opera star, like fellow athletes Drake Hogestyn, Josh Taylor, Andrew Shue, Jack Wagner, D.J. Lockhart-Johnson, John Bolger, and Eric Braeden. We have already discussed Michael Landon, a javelin thrower from USC who played Hoss Cartwright's younger brother, Joe.

Other college football players on TV and in the movies include Fess Parker. A former football player for Hardin Simmons University, in Texas, he played "Davey Crockett" in the movies and "Daniel Boone" on television. Professional football lineman Rosie Greer often played a character role with Parker, as Daniel Boone. According to his obituary (Legacy.com), Parker played for HSU in 1946. When he was injured by a road-rage stabbing, he later said "there goes m football career", and he transferred to the University of Texas where he graduated in 1950. A few years later a famous western star played football for the other major state university in Texas, called Texas A&M. His name was Ty Hardin (briansdrivein-theater.com, 1999). However, you should not try to look up his name on the Texas A&M roster, as Hardin is not his original name. Rosie was also known as a discus thrower at Penn State University.

After his pro career he also played in many movies, such as The Man with two Heads, with fellow Pennsylvania track athlete, Bruce Dern. Hugh Beaumont, the man we all know as Ward Cleaver, from the TV series "Leave it to Beaver", played football for the University of Tennessee at Chattanooga (Beaumont, 2007). Mr. Cleaver always had a calm way of reminiscing about his football days. Of course, the actor playing this role had a background that made it easy. Jack Lord (Hawaii Five-O) played football for New York University during the early 1950s (Vallance, 1998, Jan 23), beginning his acting career playing action roles, such as the TV show Stoney Burke, where he played a professional rodeo cowboy. James Caan played football for Michigan State University, and was also a Rodeo Cowboy (Caan, 2013). Years later, he would play one of the most memorable characters to play football for the Chicago Bears. In the movie "Brian's Song", Caan played Brian Piccolo, the fullback for the team, who died of cancer, at the peak of his career. This was a compelling movie that required someone that could play the role of a great football player. No one could have played the role better than James Caan. He was also very convincing as the head football coach in "The Program."

Burt Reynolds played running-back for Florida State University. He was quite good and expected to play professional football before an injury ended that choice. His football background has been reviewed on several talk shows. In fact, his teammate at FSU was sports anchor and former coach, Lee Corso. Although he is best known for his role in "Smokey and the Bandit", Burt has played a football player or a coach in other roles. He had a TV series called "Evening Shade", where he played a former football player who becomes a high school football coach. He also led the field in another popular movie about a prison football team. This movie included several fellow college and professional football players. This movie, of course, was "The Longest Yard", and one of the other actors in the movie played football for FSU shortly after

Burt. His name was Sonny Shroyer. While Sonny is best known as Enos, of "The Dukes of Hazard", he also played another football role, as "Bear" Bryant in the movie, "Forrest Gump".

A few years after "Enos" left FSU; Robert Urick played tight end for the team. Shortly, after graduate school, Robert began acting in the popular TV series, "Soap". He had a successful career in several movies, as well as starring roles on TV shows such as "Vegas", and "The Lazarus Man", as well as the popular mini-series, Lonesome Dove (Urick, 2013). Another TV icon named Lee Majors played for Eastern Kentucky University. He is best known for starring roles on "The Big Valley", "The Six Million Dollar Man", and "The Fall Guy". During the 1980s, I received my Masters degree from EKU during the time Lee's son was in school there. I also know older EKU students who played ball with Mr. Majors. Of course, I would have to look up the correct spelling of his birth name, as it is reportedly the reason he did not use it in Hollywood. I think it is spelled Yeary, or something like that. It begins and ends with a "Y".

Like Dean Cain, another football player from the Ivy League, was Tommy Lee Jones (Lonesome Dove, The Fugitive, Men In Black), who is quite well known for playing offensive line for Harvard University. Jones, of course, is also famous for being the college roommate of former Vice President Al Gore and actor John Lithgow. He was such a good athlete, that as a middle-aged man, he not only did most of his own riding stunts in Lonesome Dove, but he had to be asked to let the stuntman do the bucking bronc scenes, as he wanted to do those as well.

Fellow Tennesseans Jack Hanna (Jack Hanna's Animal Adventures) and Miles O'Keeffe (Tarzan) also played college football. Hanna left east Tennessee to play football at Muskingum College, in Ohio, where he married one of the cheerleaders. He is well known for having a pet donkey that became the mascot for Muskingum sports teams. I don't know if he planned to go to college in Ohio to become a zoo director, but it seemed to work out that way. West Tennessee resident, Miles O'Keeffe played football for Mississippi State University (Brainsdriveintheater.com, 1999). While O'Keeffe played the role of Tarzan, Hanna is sometimes referred to as a real Tarzan-type character. Two other TV and movie stars played college football next door to Hanna and O'Keefe, in Alabama. Johnny Mack Brown, best known for those old western movies, was an All-American half-back for University of Alabama, and MVP of the 1926 Rose Bowl, who turned down professional football for the stage. While he starred in many movies, he also co-starred in other westerns with John Wayne. Like Randolph Scott, who played football at Georgia Tech, Brown holds one of the three photo positions on the University of Alabama's website of notable alumni. George Lindsey, who is best known as Goober Pyle on the "Andy Griffith Show" played quarterback for University of North Alabama. He was also a biology teacher before becoming "Goober". As a college professor in Tennessee, I often have fun talking about George with my friends who are teachers from northern Alabama.

An actor, who became a household name, playing a role similar to George Lindsey, was a college football player at the University of Idaho. The role as "Dauber" in the TV series "Coach" will always make Bill Fagerbakke a TV icon. Although, he is still a major movie star, his voice is currently known, internationally, in the role as "Patrick Star" on the TV series (and movie), "SpongeBob Square-Pants". At a large 6'6", Fagerbakke could have been a professional athlete. Although, a knee injury ended his football career while he was in college, his deep heavy voice has made him millions on television and in the movies (Starpulse.com, 2008). Another football player whose athletic career ended with an injury was Dr. Phil, who played football for University of Tulsa. Another large, fit man, Dr. Phil is a psychologist who has an athletic presence on his TV show (Wikipedia.org, 2013).

Craig Sheffer played college football and baseball at East Stroudsburg State University, in Pennsylvania (TCM.com). He played many different types of roles in movies such as "A River Runs through It", and currently co-stars on the TV series, "One Tree Hill". However, like Burt Reynolds, and other actors who had carried the "pig skin", Craig's football background made him very convincing when he played a college football quarterback in the movie called "The Program". Co-starring with former college football player James Caan, The Program, was a movie that required some athletes-turned-actors to form a credible movie about college football.

Soap opera star Josh Taylor played quarterback for Dartmouth University during the 1960s when they were the Ivy League Champions, before going to law school. After becoming a lawyer he became a popular TV star in several roles, before playing his current role as Roman Brady in the popular soap opera "Days of Our Lives". Roman Brady is actually the second starring-role he has played on the series (Wikipedia.org, 2013). Another interesting point about this role that relates to another athlete in this book is that it is the same role that was previously played by former professional baseball player Drake Hogestyn, who became a popular star on the same show, as another character named John Black (Wikipedia.org, 2013). This relationship seems to be a major theme of the show. However, you will have to watch the show to understand more about it.

Other soap opera stars include former Bucknell University Linebacker, John Bolger. As one of the stars of "Guiding Light", he often shares the stage with former NFL great Mark Schlereth. During the late 1980s, DJ Lockhart-Johnson was one of the best defensive backs in the history of the University of Kentucky, before he began his NFL career with the Pittsburg Steelers, in 1989. He currently stars as Coleman "Doc" Reese, on "As the World Turns".

One of the more unique athletes in this book is John "Bradshaw" Layfield. He played college football at Abilene Christian University, followed by two professional USFL teams, then becoming a professional wrestler. Using his initials, JBL, as his wrestling persona, he is still a popular professional wrestler. However, he has become a popular financial contributor on the Fox Business New Network, and has his own radio show on hundreds of stations.

There is no shortage of professional football players that later became TV and movie stars. Some of these athletes include Mike Henry (Tarzan), Terry Crews (Everybody Hates Chris), Ed Marinaro (Hill Street Blues), Fred Dreyer (Hunter), Same J. Jones (Flash Gordon), Ben Davidson (Conan The Barbarian), and John Matuszak (Sloth, from "The Goonies"), Eric Alan Kramer (Robin Hood, Men in Tights), Bernie Casey (Felix, in Never Say Never Again), Jim Brown (Dirty Dozen) Merlin Olson (Little House on the Prairie), Roman Gabriel (The Undefeated, with Merlin Olson), Howie Long (Monday Night Football), Carl Weathers (Rocky), Fred Williamson (Starsky and Hutch), O. J. Simpson (several movies), Tim Rossovich (character actor in many movies and TV shows) and Alan Autry (Bubba Skinner, from "In The Heat Of The Night"). Autry has been the Mayor of Fresno, California for several years. Of course, we have to mention Joe Namath who played professional football as the quarterback for the New York Jets, and is the other football player illustrated next to Johnny Mack Brown on the website for the University of Alabama. Each of these athletes has starred in many movies, but is probably best remembered for the ones named in this paragraph. A semi-pro football player named Forrest Tucker (2013) has a long career in movies, playing in multiple movies with fellow football player, John Wayne, in westerns as well as war movies. He also played the father of five sport champion, Bo Svenson, in Walking Tall. However, he is probably best known for his role in TV shows such as "F-Troop".

It is not surprising that many of these athletes-turned-actors made movies about football. Mike Henry played in "The Longest Yard", while Terry Crews and Brian Bosworth played in the remake of "The Longest Yard", in 2005. Brian Dennehy played in Semi-Tough, while John Matuszak and Alan Autry were each in "North Dallas Forty". However, former Green Bay Packer quarterback, Alan Autry is best known for the role of Bubba Skinner, in the long-running TV series, "In the Heat of the Night". In this series, his character was a police officer who also coached the local high school football team.

Many movies are made about football, utilizing former college athletes, as well. In "The Longest Yard", the leading role was played by former FSU running back, Burt Reynolds. Another FSU football player named Sonny Shroyer also played a role in this movie. Another of the athletes in "North Dallas Forty", and the second tallest leading man of the 1970s, was Bo Svenson. Rather than being labeled as a college athlete, this multi-sport, world-class athlete is also an adjunct college professor.

We have already discussed how Matthew Fox played the role of Coach Dawson in "We Are Marshall", Sonny Shroyer played the role of Coach Bryant, in "Forrest Gump", and Craig Sheffer played a Heisman trophy candidate in "The Program". Although, Herman Brix (stage name was Bruce Bennett) is best known for being the silver medalist in the shot put, during the 1928 Olympics, he also played college football player at the University of Washington, when they played against Alabama in the 1926 Rose Bowl. One of his first movie roles in the early 1930s, was entitled, "Touchdown". However, another injury among these athletes took place during the filming of this movie, and Brix had to turn down the role of Tarzan, The Ape Man. Therefore, Olympic swimmer, Johnny Weissmuller took the role, and became the most famous actor to play Tarzan, playing this role in twelve movies. During the auditions, Johnny was asked if he could run. He replied, yeah, I can run. However, MGM decided that they would need to add more swimming scenes because of Weissmuller. A few years later, Brix would play the role of Tarzan, as well. Before we heard the Tarzan yells from Brix and Weissmuller, Edgar Rice Burroughs, the author of the Tarzan books discovered an All-American Football player from Indiana University named James Pierce. As a muscular 6'4", Burroughs thought he would be ideal for the 1927 role, in a silent movie. Pierce had been a high school football coach at Glendale, where he coached future celebrities such as John Wayne. Pierce married Burroughs daughter, Joan.

A unique relationship that can be made about Herman Brix is that while he was playing tackle for the University of Washington, he played in the 1926 Rose Bowl against the University of Alabama, where an All-American half-back named Johnny Mack Brown was playing. Brown was the MVP in that Rose Bowl. After Alabama won the Rose Bowl, Brown turned down professional football to become one of the biggest cowboy stars in the movies. Several movie stars of the old westerns were college football players. Around the time when Brix and Brown were playing college football, western movie star Charles Starrett began playing football for Dartmouth, before soap star and former Dartmouth QB Josh Taylor was born (Charles Starrett, 2012).

Of course, many of the professional football players competed against each other on a regular basis. However, some of them share some more unique relationships. While Fred Dryer was playing for the Los Angeles Rams and Carl Weathers was playing for the Oakland Raiders, they would be rivals. However, when they played college ball for San Diego State University, they were teammates. Weathers began playing for the Raiders shortly after former Raider Fred Williamson retired from the Chiefs and began playing in the movies during the late 1960s.

Another interesting relationship was Tom Selleck's college roommate, Timothy John Rossovich, who of course played college football for USC, followed by many years in the NFL, playing for the Chargers, Eagles and Oilers before playing roles in Magnum PI, with his roommate, as well as movies. His younger brother Rick was also a college athlete who made many movies, especially action roles such as Navy Seals, and The Lords of Discipline, as the roommate of the former manager for the University of Tennessee football team, David Keith. Keith is well known in Tennessee, as he is the former manager for the UT football team and lives near his home town in east Tennessee where he can often be seen on the field during UT football games.

Before John Layfield and Kevin Nash were multi-sport professional wrestlers, another professional wrestler, named Woody Strode was a UCLA decathlete, before becoming one of the first two African-Americans to play professional football for the Rams during the late 1940s (Woody Strode, 2013). Mark Harmon's father, Tom Harmon, would have played for the Rams during this time. After leaving the Rams, he became a popular professional wrestler, before he made his mark in the movies. He often played action roles, even when he had reached the age of sixty. As a very fit man, he was quite well known for roles where he did not wear a shirt. He often played the villain in Tarzan movies, or as a Native-American, in westerns. Of course, in Sergeant Rutledge, he played an army sergeant in the old west and one of his soldiers was played by Rafer Johnson. Since the movie was filmed in 1960, it would have been shortly after Johnson won the Olympic Decathlon, and perhaps his first role in a movie. But we will talk about Johnson later in this book. We have also mentioned a football player named Jim Brown, who was thought to be one of the greatest football players to play the game. However, before he played for the Cleveland Browns, with fellow decathlete Milt Campbell, we placed in the top five, as a teenager at the 1955 National Decathlon Championships, next to Rafer Johnson. Like Johnson and Strode, he was also a multi-talented athlete, who played basketball and lacrosse as well.

It may not come as a surprise to find out the number of college athletes, especially football players that went into other professions, or transferred to other colleges because of an injury. We have already mentioned several. John Wayne got into the movies after a surfing accident caused him to lose his football scholarship. A more recent occasion involved Daniel Cudmore, an athletic 6'8" football player at Gannon University in Pennsylvania. With his massive physique, he may have had a promising career in professional football. However, shortly after his injury, he was offered the role of Colossus, in two of the X-Men movies (Cudmore, 2013). Other football players such as Randolph Scott, transferred to UNC in his home state of North Carolina, after an injury ended his football career at Georgia Tech. Likewise, after an injury, Sonny Shroyer lost his football scholarship at FSU, and returned to his home state of Georgia to finish his business degree at the University of Georgia. This may have been his best career move. While attending UGA, his picture was seen on a football program, and he was offered many other commercial modeling jobs that helped his career in TV and movies. Dr. Phil played football for the University of Tulsa before being injured. However, he transferred to Midwestern State University, in Texas, to finish his degree, and continued his education in order to become the famous TV personality we see today. Dean Cain made the NFL team, the Buffalo Bills, before a knee injury ended his football career, and he became the TV superman of the 1990s. Jock Mahoney's (Tarzan, Range Rider) football career ended when World War II began. The war began after he graduated from the University of Iowa, returning from the war as the top stuntman in Hollywood, followed by movies and TV series. Hugh Beaumont (Ward Cleaver) transferred from the University of Tennessee at Chattanooga to the University of Southern California, after a change in the UTC football strategy discontinued his playing position (IMDb.com, 2007).

An injury in sport is often the best thing that ever happened to an athlete that is more gifted in another sport or another profession. We have named a few in this book. If Bruce Jenner had not been injured in football, he may have never been "the world's greatest athlete", in the 1976 Olympics, or a TV star, on ChiPs, and now The Kardasians. As strange as this may sound, athletes often receive injuries that keep them from playing particular sports, without having a disabling injury. A 1980 movie, entitled, "The Golden Moment" starred former University of Tennessee football manager, David Keith, as a college football player, on his way to the NFL, who is injured, and unable to accept a professional football contract. However, like Jenner, he is still a great athlete, and becomes the silver medalist in the 1980 Olympics (the Olympics boycotted by the U.S.). The actor playing David's father, was Jack Palance, a former professional boxer whose boxing career was ended when WWII began. He was severely injured during the war, as well. Oddly enough, Jack became recognized as a movie star when he, accidently, injured another movie star, named Marlon Brando.

In a sport like steer wrestling, a knee injury is a "death sentence", but Brad Johnson's athletic physique made him one of the most recognized men in modeling, and acting. While Drake Hogestyn may have been looking to television as something for the "off season", an injury would make it his career. Kurt Russell has been interviewed on the subject, and makes no pretense about it. If he had not been injured, he would have stayed in professional baseball and never returned to the movies. Whether or not an athlete is injured, or left professional sports to chase other goals after reaching all of them in sport, the positive characteristics that made them great athletes, make them successful in other parts of their lives, as illustrated by these exceptional men. Many football fans have different views concerning the reason All-pro football player; Gayle Sayers left the Chicago Bears, at the height of his career. However, in a TV interview, he explained that he had reached all of his goals in football. Therefore, he wanted to reach his goals in business. Today, he is a very successful businessman. This unselfish, ambitious behavior gave Archie "Moonlight" Graham's home town a superior doctor, the United States several enlightened presidents, and the world many talented entertainers.

We often see professional wrestlers on the big screen. While Hulk Hogan (Terry Bollea) is probably best know for making several movies, most of us can remember Jesse "The Body" Ventura in "Predator", Paul "Big Show" White in "The Waterboy", or Andrea the Giant in "The Princess Bride". Who recognized Randy "Macho Man" Savage in the movie "Spiderman"? Most recently, a 6'10" wrestler named Tyler Mane has become quite popular, playing in action movies. He was Ajax in the movie "Troy", and Sabertooth in "The X-Men". As tall, athletic men, these athletes usually have another athletic background, as well. For example, Mark Calaway (The Undertaker) a 6'10" wrestler played basketball for Angelina College, in Texas, and Kevin Nash, another 6'10" wrestler played college and professional basketball. "El Egante" at 7'8" was a member of his country's Olympic basketball team. He has often been seen playing monsters in the on TV and/or movies, as well as giants in movies such as Hercules, and Zorro, a fitting role for a 7'8" man, with a muscular frame. Dwayne "The Rock" Johnson played football for the University of Miami, and John "Bradshaw" Layfield played college and professional football.

People are often surprised when they find out the "super intelligence" possessed by most of these guys. Many of the professional wrestlers are former doctors, lawyers, teachers and college professors. When a popular cartoon was developed for TV about some of the top professional wrestlers of the 1980s, one of them was "Hillbilly Jim". At roughly, 6'8", and 300 pounds, he wore a long beard, bibbed overhauls, and a "hillbilly hat". He also wore a horseshoe on a chain, around his neck, and carried a pig. However, this guy had a master's degree in education, and taught high school in Bowling Green, Kentucky. Of course, we can't forget Mike Mazurki, the 6'5" professional wrestler we remember from movies in the 1960s such as Bull Whip Griffin and many other movies and

TV shows where he was portrayed as a lowbrow thug. However, Mike was really a very intelligent conversationalist. Mike was another one of those athletes-turned-actor that we saw in so many TV shows that made you say "hey, that's what's his name".

John Payne has been a well known actor since the 1930s, and no one would be surprised that he worked as a singer during college. However, some of his fans may be surprised to also know that he worked his way through college as a boxer and a wrestler. Shorty after graduating from Columbia University, in 1930, he began a successful career in film (briansdriveintheater.com, 1999).

In 1948, Congressman Bob Mathias was the youngest American track athlete to win the gold medal in the Olympics. As a decathlete, this was especially amazing. He won two gold medals at a younger age than most decathletes begin to be successful. While a movie about his life, viewed much of the Olympic Games, it did not include footage of the 1948 Olympic Trials, when he won it shortly after finishing high school. If it had, we would have seen a young athlete taking sixth place in the decathlon, and finishing first in the 1500, the last of the ten events (Track & Field News, 1948). His name was Dennis Weaver, a man who later became a major TV and movie star in such roles as McCloud, as well as the well known character, "Chester" on the long running series, Gunsmoke. Oddly enough, athletes are often chosen to play roles, like "Chester", that require the actor to perform a disability. Matthew Fox played a similar role that required him to move differently than most people, as well. This type of role is not as easy as it may seem.

Several Olympic decathletes have made movies. Bruce Jenner won the gold medal in the 1976 Olympics. Afterwards, he played in movies and TV roles such as CHiPs. He was also a college football player. Glen Morris, the 1936 Olympic decathlon champion, played Tarzan, shortly after he returned from the Olympics and also played professional football. Rafer Johnson, the 1960 Olympic champion, often played a villain in the Tarzan movies with pro football star, Mike Henry who played the role of Tarzan. Johnson went on to play many other movie roles, as well.

Rafer Johnson was also a college decathlete, as well as a basketball player, for UCLA. About twenty years earlier, another UCLA decathlete named Woody Strode would play villains in several Tarzan movies, after becoming one of the first African-Americans to play professional football, for the Rams, during the late 1940s, followed by several years as a professional wrestler, before playing many supporting roles in action movies. Strode and Johnson also joined forces in 1960, when they shared the screen in the first movie where we saw Rafer Johnson.

Another track and field athlete who played in Tarzan movies was Herman Brix (stage name Bruce Bennett) who was the silver medalist in the shot put, in the 1928 Olympics. He went on to play in many westerns, in his later years. As a middle-aged man he teamed up in a western with an Olympic swimmer who played Tarzan named Buster Crabbe. Track athletes seemed to do well in Tarzan movies.

Many TV and movie stars were track & field athletes during college, as well as in the Olympics. Weight throwers tend to do well as action heroes. We have already mentioned that Herman Brix threw the shot put in the Olympics. Another famous actor named Clancy Brown threw the discus for Northwestern University. While playing many roles in Starship Troopers, Earth II, and The Guardian, and the Frankenstein creature in The Bride, he is probably best known as Kurgan, in The Highlander. Clancy has several unique relationships with other athletes in this book. One unique relationship we could make, concerning this athlete, is that he is the son of Ohio Congressman Clarence Brown Jr., and the grandson of Ohio Congressman Clarence Brown. Although, the Brown family is from Ohio, Clancy's father was a congressman, and he graduated from St. Albans Prep School, in Washington D.C., where Vice President Al Gore had played high school football and basketball, and also threw the discus, during the 1960s, about 15 years before Brown. A third relationship would be his many voices in video games and his role as the voice of Mr. Krabbs, on "SpongeBob Squarepants". (StarPulse.com, 2008). He shared the "audio stage" on SpongeBob Squarepants, with Bill Fagerbakke, (eternally known for his role as Dauber, in TV's Coach) a football player who graduated from the University of Idaho, in 1981, the same year Brown graduated from Northwestern. It has to be interesting to watch these two very large, athletic men, when they are speaking the roles of these cartoon characters. Like Bill, Clancy is well-known for his many animated characters.

While being large men may have helped most throwers to get acting roles in action movies, at least one of them was a relatively average sized man. Michael Landon (Bonanza, and Little House on the Prairie) was a champion javelin thrower who went to the University of Southern California, on a track & field scholarship, before beginning his acting career as a "Teenage Werewolf". Bill Cosby ran track for Temple University, in his home town of Philadelphia. Growing up in the town where he competed in college, he competed in the Penn Relays, every year from the time he was 12 years old, through middle age. He even filmed at least one of his 1990s TV shows with the theme of the Masters Mile Relay event at the Penn Relays. He also played football and basketball in college. Cosby is also an accomplished tennis player, a sport in which pop music star Lionel Ritchie played for Tuskegee University, in Alabama.

Another track athlete who competed in the Penn Relays was Bruce Dern. Interestingly, he has several relationships with other athletes in this book. Like Bill Cosby, he ran in the Penn Relays; like Senator Bob Dole, he ran the half-mile; and like Michael Landon, there was an issue with his hair. According to the New York Times (1996, April 21), Ken Doherty (the 1928 Olympic Decathlete), his coach kicked him off the team because he would not cut his long, hair. While we have discussed Dern and Penn State discus thrower, Rosie Greer, playing the two heads of The Two Headed Man, one more relationship he has with other track athletes in this book is one the shares with Clancy Brown. He is the grandson of a famous politician. His grandfather was a former governor of Utah, as well as a former U.S. secretary of war. Clancy Brown is the son, as well as the grandson of U.S. congressmen, from Ohio.

Of course, no book about athletes on stage would be complete without talking about Marty Glickman, the 1936 Olympic sprinter and Syracuse University football standout who along with the only other Jewish member of the track team was replaced with Jesse Owens and Ralph Metcalfe in the 400 meter relay. Glickman became on one of the foremost sports announcers and received a metal years later by the Olympic Committee in 1998, two years before he died. At 18 years old, about the only champion track athlete that was younger than he was would have been fellow Marine, Bob Mathias. Another relationship that Glickman held with other track athletes and football players in this book is fellow Syracuse football player Jim Brown who was a track & field standout as a teenager.

If we discussed the many entertainers that were high school track athletes, we would find some of them that are quite surprising. For example, rock star Alice Cooper was an undefeated distance runner during his senior year of high school. Another rock star known as Sting was an undefeated sprinter. And we could include another high school track athlete who played in Several Tarzan movies, during the 1950s, named Lex Barker. However, if we include many high school athletes, we would need to include a great high school swimmer named Viggo Mortensen Lord of the Rings), as well as wrestlers Robin Williams (who also ran track), St. X wrestler, Tom Cruise, and Glen Frey (The Eagles).

As mentioned in several areas of this book, Bo Svenson was a world class athlete in many sports, including track & field. As a multisport athlete, Bo played in many action movies. However, he is probably best known for his role as Buford Pusser, in the true story about the sheriff that fought against organized crime in a small town in Tennessee.

Another sport where we often find actors to play in Tarzan movies is swimming. Johnny Weissmuller was the most popular character to play this role. He was a multi-gold medalist in more than one Olympic Games. Weissmuller was such an exceptional athlete that he did very unusual things and still won gold medals. For example, according to a biographical book, written several years ago, about one of Johnny's fellow Olympians, during the 1928 Olympics, it was time for one of Johnny's events. However, no one could find him. Suddenly one of his friends said she knew where he was. So she ran to the café and found him eating a pizza and two hot dogs. She told him that he did not have time to eat before his event. Nevertheless, he gobbled down the pizza and picked up the two hot dogs and ran to the pool. Then he ate both hot dogs, dove in the pool and won the gold medal. After playing Tarzan for nearly 20 years, he started another well known series called Jungle Jim.

Shortly after Johnny became Tarzan, another Olympic swimming champion named Larry "Buster" Crabbe put on the loin cloth. Buster was a very unique athlete. After playing in a couple of Tarzan movies, he became the star of serials such as Flash Gordon, and Buck Rogers. During his 50s, he returned to the role of Tarzan. One of his last TV appearances, before his death, was as a guest star in the 1980s version of Buck Rogers, the character he had made popular 40 years earlier. During the late 1970s many new movies were made about comic book heroes from the past. The new generation of action heroes brought us a re-make of Flash Gordon. In this movie, the character made famous by Buster Crabbe, was played by former NFL wide receiver Sam J. Jones.

During the 1960s a college swimmer from the University of Iowa, named Jock Mahoney played the role of Tarzan. Jock was an incredible athlete who played college football and basketball, as well. Like Burt Lancaster and Clayton Moore, he began his acting career as a stuntman. He worked as a stunt double for some of the biggest stars in Hollywood, including John Wayne. In 1948, he doubled for Errol Flynn, in a movie where he had to jump from roof top to roof top, and jumping down a staircase in one step, while fencing. He always made difficult stunts look easy, as he leaped on his horse, during westerns without appearing to be stressed while doing the stunt. He did his own stunts in Tarzan movies, and reportedly, could hop across a horse. This ability would obviously, get him roles in westerns. In fact, he was best known for his role as the "Range Rider". He actually, played the role of Tarzan during his early to mid forties. He was named as the oldest actor to play the role of Tarzan (the first time). When actress Sally Field said that her step-father was "bigger than life" she was talking about Jock Mahoney. The stories about men who played Tarzan can be located in many different sites. A few years ago, AMC ran a series of Tarzan movies throughout the weekend. Since Brandon Frazer had recently played George of the Jungle in the movies, he narrated the entire series, including some interesting such pieces of information during his narration. Other documentaries have been made about the Tarzan character as well. We discussed how former UCLA basketball player Denny Miller told children that if he gave his Tarzan yell, animals would stampede. One particular book about afore mentioned Herman Brix was entitled Please Don't Call me Tarzan, probably because he looked so much like the character. With a few exceptions, most of the actors that played Tarzan were close to the same size, and several of them were great swimmers.

Other aquatic athletes in the movies include Ester Williams, who became a star in the World's Fair when Johnny Weissmuller left. We have already talked about Fox News anchor Laurie Dhue, who was a swimmer at the University of North Carolina.

Kim Alexis, another TV host and model, was a great high school swimmer. During the 1960s, women would watch a muscular TV doctor named Ben Casey. The actor who played the role was a former swimmer at Ohio State University named Vince Edwards (Briansdriveintheater.org, 1999). Ted McGinley, co-star of "Married with Children", "Happy Days", and "Faith and Hope", has also played in many movies, such as "Revenge of the Nerds". He was also the captain of his college water polo team (TV.com, 2008). Jason Statham (The Transporter, and The Bank Job) was a British Olympic Diver, before his kick boxing skills help to land him roles in many action films (Wikipedia.org, 2013). Perhaps, one of the greatest women to swim in the Olympics was Eleanor Holms Jarrett. As the world record holder in the back stroke, she won a gold medal in the 1928 Olympics. As a famous movie star and an out-spoken young lady, during a time when Olympic curfews were quite strict, she was dropped from the 1936 team after a party and a remark that she trained on caviar and champagne, on board the SS Manhattan which was the ship that transported the U.S. Olympic team to Germany. However, immediately after the 1936 Olympics, she was chosen to play the role of Jane in Tarzan's Revenge, with 1936 Olympic decathlon champion, Glen Morris. She was also allowed to use her own first name in this movie. Years later, she was interviewed during the Olympic Games. She reportedly stated that she still liked champagne.

Since rowing is the oldest sponsored college sport in the U.S., we need to add some other athletes who spent their college years moving across the water such as a Georgetown University crew athlete named Bradley Cooper. The 1997 graduate rowed for GU during the mid 1990s and became an actor before graduation. Since then, he has played in many diverse roles as leading men, as well as character roles, in movies such as Wedding Crashers, Hangover I and II, The A-team. Other crew athletes include Gregory Peck, who rowed for the University of California – Berkeley, Vincent Price and Edward Norton rowed at Yale, and Anderson Cooper coxed for Yale (rowinghistory.net). Since they are close to the same age, Norton would have rowed at Yale during the late 1980s during the time Anderson Cooper coxed for the team (Rowinghistory. net, 2013). You may recognize that many of these celebrities are quite tall. Although there are two weight classes in rowing, athletes in the heavier 8-man class have an average height similar to that of a basketball team.

Probably the most famous entertainer from a professional boxing background went by the boxing name of "Packy East". However, most of us know him as Bob Hope, who was also known as one of the best golfers in Hollywood. Tony Danza was another professional boxer who made it big on TV and in the movies (Wikipedia.org., 2013). In his first major role as a taxi driver in the TV series named Taxi, he also got to play the role of a boxer. News anchor and TV show host, Geraldo Rivera boxed at the University of Arizona.

Boxing is a sport that is valuable to action heroes on television, and in the movies. Robert Conrad, primarily known for his action hero role in the Wild Wild West, illustrated his prowess as a former professional boxer. Reb Brown was the heavyweight that got to use his boxing abilities often as an action hero. He is most fondly remembered for two movies, during the late 1970s and early 1980s, where he played the role of comic book hero Captain America. He actually looked like the comic book character. As a multi-talented athlete, Reb also played football for USC (Briansdriveintheater. com, 1999). Former heavyweight champion Max Baer played in a couple of movies. However, his brother Buddy, at over 6'6", and thought to be the hardest puncher in professional boxing during the late 1930s and 40s, left his boxing career to be in several movies with Abbott and Costello, as well as The Three Stooges. He is probably best known for his role in Quo Vadis, where he was a former gladiator-turned-Christian, who had to kill a bull in the arena by breaking its neck. Max Baer also trained his son to be a boxer. However, after one boxing match during college, Max Baer Jr. suffered a technical knock-out during the first round, and he decided that boxing would not be his profession. Shortly after graduating from college, he became a household name as Jethro, on the popular TV series, The Beverly Hillbillies.

Like Bo Svenson, actor William Smith (2013), was a multi-sport athlete while serving in the military service. He was a champion boxer, weight-lifter, body builder, and an arm wrestling champion, as well as a semi-pro football player. While he has played in several movie and TV roles, he is probably best known for his role as "Joe Riley" in the 1960s, TV series, "Laredo", where the plot of the show often found ways to portray him without a shirt. One professional boxer-turned-actor who competed in more sports than perhaps, anyone in this book was Dale Robertson. Since he was a professional boxer after he graduated from high school, although, he was recruited by universities all over the country, he would not have been able to compete in an NCAA supported university, so he turned down the chance to play football at major universities and attended Oklahoma Military Academy where he earned 32 awards in boxing, football, baseball, tennis, polo and swimming, and was named all-round outstanding athlete (Seldon, 1992, June 11). While he played in many movies, he is best known for his TV series, "Tales of Wells Fargo".

One of the reasons there were so many good fight scenes in the westerns during the 1940s, 50s and 60s was that so many of the leading men and villains were boxers. Another actor known for making westerns, named George O'Brien, was a navy boxer who also became a heavy-weight champion (Briansdriveintheater. com, 1999). Western movie star George Montgomery boxed while attending the University of Montana before turning professional as a heavyweight (Briansdriveintheater.com, 1999). Richard Boone (Have Gun, Will Travel), was on the boxing team at Stanford University before becoming a professional boxer

(Richard Boone, 2009). Like many athletes in his generation, his boxing career ended when he joined the military, during World War II. Dale Robertson served in WWII as a tank commander, before sharing the western TV serials of the 1960s, with fellow boxer Richard Boone. Like Boone, 1930s Dartmouth Heavyweight Boxing champion, Robert Ryan played villains in many westerns (Robert Ryan, 2013).

As explained earlier, large athletes often play villains in the movies. At 6'6", former heavyweight contender Jack O'Halloran is no different. After winning most of his fights during the late 1960s and early 1970s, being defeated by Heavyweight Champion George Foreman, he moved on to the movies. He is probably best known as a villain in Superman I and II and Emil Muzz in Dragnet (O'Halloron, 2013). Character actors like O'Halloran and Baer often "laugh all the way to the bank" while someone else takes center-stage in the movie. Heavyweight boxer Tex Cobb has played many such roles.

A unique story of a boxers who became actors, is the one about Mickey Rourke. After growing up boxing, he became a famous actor, at a young age. However, at the age of 33, he became a professional boxer (Wikipedia.org, 2013). He returned to acting in his late 30s, and recently starred in an award-winning movie called The Wrestler, where he plays a professional wrestler who is in his late 50s, an age when most men in the profession have been retired for a long time. Someone who had began a boxing career when most boxers were retiring who have a great insight for playing this role.

Perhaps the best story of a boxer becoming a famous actor has to be Jack Palance, a heavy weight who fought under the name Jack Brazzo. He originally left the mining towns of Pennsylvania to play football for the University of North Carolina. Like Boone and Robertson, his professional boxing career ended when he joined the military to fight in WWII. After the war, he was an understudy for Marlin Brando (Jack Palance, 2013). Although, he was longer a professional boxer, he still trained like one. While he was working out on the heavy bag, he accidently "punched out" Brando, putting him in the hospital. As Brando's understudy, Jack had to replace him in a show, where he became a star. Much later in life, he would make a very funny joke about it, when he received his last Oscar, during the Academy Awards.

When talking about movies, obviously many stars of westerns would include former (and current) rodeo stars. From the beginning of the westerns, stars like Tom Mix and Hoot Gibson were former rodeo cowboys. A child trick rider in the rodeo with Hoot Gibson named Dick Jones became a famous TV star in the first westerns during the 1950s as Buffalo Bill Jr. and Joch Mahoney's sidekick in The range Rider (Wikipedia.org, 2013). Slim Pickens, Ken Curtis, and Ben Johnson left the rodeo for the stage, and in the next generation, steer wrestler, Brad Johnson, and bronc rider, Ron White would join this club. While model and movie star Brad Johnson may be an obvious transition, Ron White is well known as a comedian, who often refers to his background in rodeo on stage. While some may wonder about the transition from the rodeo to comedy, it was good training for rodeo star-turned-movie star Slim Pickens. Slim Pickens got his name from the rodeo, as a teenager, when he won his first major paycheck and someone said there would be "slim pickens" out there today (Wikipedia.org., 2013). After spending several years as a rodeo cowboy, he became a well-respected rodeo clown, which may have helped him in the many comedy roles he would play later in the movies. A saddle bronc rider, in the rodeo, named Hank Worden, often played comic relief characters in the movies, as well, often playing in roles with John Wayne, and fellow rodeo cowboy, Ken Curtis. Ken Curtis had an interesting career as a musician and a rodeo cowboy, before becoming a house-hold name as "Festus", on the long running TV show, Gunsmoke. He replaced former All-American decathlete

Dennis Weaver, who played "Chester" during the previous eleven years (Track & Field News, 1948).

Other stories include Tom Mix going from the rodeo, to the movies, and then to the circus. Mix is portrayed in the movie Sunset, performing his many stunts on a horse. However, another rodeo cowboy was not primarily remembered for his western movies. While he played in many westerns including one of his first movies called Journey to Shiloh, he is best known for movies such as Misery, as well as Brian's Song, where he did not play a cowboy. However, Michigan State University football player and movie star, James Caan was also a professional rodeo cowboy. A semi-professional football player for the Oklahoma City Driller, a USFL farm team, named Toby Keith, was also a rodeo cowboy, before he recorded his first hit song, "Should've been a Cowboy" (TV.com, 2008). Since then, Toby has sold millions of recordings, but still raises horses on his ranch.

Perhaps, one of the best stories of a rodeo cowboy becoming an actor is the one about Ben Johnson. He was a rodeo cowboy for several years before becoming a movie star. About ten years later, he returned to the rodeo and became a world champion, before returning to the movies. Brad Johnson (model and movie star) started as a baseball player at Oregon State University, then a rodeo athlete at the University of Southern Idaho, followed by years of wrestling steers on the professional rodeo circuit until a knee injury ended his athletic career and he became an actor. He is often seen as a supporting actor, but also plays leading men. In fact, he can be seen in at least one movie with two other athletes named in this book, when he and Mark Harmon played villains in a Louis L'Amour movie, Crossfire Trail, against the leading man, Tom Selleck. As former models, Selleck and Johnson have similar backgrounds. According to Sanz (1990, Feb 19), Brad was raised on a cattle ranch in Arizona with a father taught him that he could accomplish anything, and Brad is proof of that. Several rodeo cowboys played in western movies, together, as well as with other athletes, in this book. Ben Johnson, Hank Worden, and James Caan, have each played in movies where the leading man was former USC football player John Wayne.

Many times people only remember rodeo cowboys as rough and tough guys. However, Reba McIntyre is definitely not a guy. A Grammy winning musician with her own TV show and many businesses in entertainment, she went to college on a rodeo scholarship. She was a barrel racer. Contrary to opinion, rodeo stars take very good care of their animals. As a graduate student at Middle Tennessee State University, my girlfriend lived near the McIntyre ranch, outside of Nashville. Once as we were driving by her home, I said that she had a beautiful home. In response, my girlfriend corrected me and said "that's not her house, that's her barn".

We have mainly been talking about Americans in this book. However, in the movies and on television several individuals from other countries have impacted our culture. One former athlete that can be seen in some of the most popular movies over the past 40 years is Sean Connery, the original James Bond. Placing third in Mr. Universe, Connery was offered the role to play Tarzan during the 1960s, shortly after he had co-starred as a villain against Gordon Scott, as Tarzan. However, most anyone who has ever watched a James Bond movie is glad that he made another choice. Not only has he made the character of James Bond into an icon, but he also establishes the idea of "growing old gracefully". Just as Buster Crabbe played Tarzan as a young man, and returned to play the role again in his 50s, Sean Connery returned to the James Bond role during his 50s, as well. He also demonstrated his athletic abilities in the movies, as a much older man, in movies such as Highlander, and The Rock. In First Knight he played King Arthur with fellow athlete Richard Gere as Sir Lancelot. Gere had attended the University of Massachusetts on a gymnastics scholarship and had the opportunity to demonstrate his gymnastic abilities in this movie, as he did in others.

Shortly after "Mr. Bond" left the sport of body building, another body builder from the British Isles became "Mr. British Isles". At approximately 6'8" and a "solid" 300 pounds, this young body builder was destined to be in the movies, while becoming the "fitness guru' of Britain. As a fitness trainer he has helped to build muscle on other famous actors, such as Christopher Reeve, when he gained weight to be a more believable Superman. However, this actor/athlete/fitness professional is mostly famous for acting roles where his face is not seen. While playing many roles as monsters in British movies, Americans know him best as "Darth Vader" in the Star Wars movies. Of course, we are talking about David Prowse.

It probably makes the "intellectual couch potatoes," sick to mention a European martial arts champion who was a genius. Most of them would think I am making up a story, when I say that the big guy who has played so many comic book characters, and the exploited Russian boxer in Rocky IV, is actually, a genius, who studied around the world, and was getting a master's degree in engineering, at one of the most academically elite universities in the world when he was asked to play the villain in Rocky IV. Of course, I am talking about Dolph Lundgren, the Swedish born actor that swept our imagination during the 80s and 90s, in such roles as He-Man, The Punisher, I Come in Peace, and The Expendables. He also made a movie about the modern pentathlon while promoting the sport around the world.

While many extra-ordinary individuals have been named in this book, another athlete who seems to capture the theme is Arnold Schwarzenegger. Anyone who has not heard his success story has probably been living in a cave. He grew up in Austria and trained with weights, for sports. This led him to become Mr. Universe. But that was not enough for someone with his drive and ambition. He wanted to be Mr. Olympia, so he moved to the United

States when he was about 20 years old. Although, his English was not very good, and he had very little money, he started a business with his friend and fellow body builder, Franco Columbo, while he trained to become the world's most famous body builder. While accomplishing these feats, he also attended college and received a business degree, became a major box-office attraction in the movies, learned to speak English, fluently, and developed one of the largest business organizations in the country, before spending two terms as the governor of California.. Today, he is one of the riches men in the world, and gives more money back to the community than most people earn. Since his involvement in the Special Olympics, he power lifting has been added which seems to have added confidence in these athletes. This concept is similar to the results of the AIMS Test that is given to Paralympics athletes, in order to determine their athletic identity. He is also a major sponsor for the Inner City Games. He is truly an athlete that has channeled his abilities into other parts of his life, in a way that has benefited many people.

As mentioned earlier, concerning wrestlers and body builders, many of them performed in the movies because of their large size. We have repeatedly mentioned another young athlete who moved to America from Sweden, as a teenager, then joined the U.S. Marines and at over 6'6", became a world class athlete in several sports, as well as becoming a TV and movie star, and university professor. This unique individual is Bo Svenson who was obviously a good choice for the role of Buford Pusser, in last two movies of the Walking Tall trilogy. Like his character, he was an athlete and a U.S. Marine. He also produces movies and writes Swedish-English lexicons. Bo was a world class athlete in track & field, judo, hockey, auto racing and yacht racing. He is especially well known as a judo champion who came back to the sport 40 years later to place in the 65-69 age- group in master's judo. Oddly enough, Svenson played in a movie about marines, entitled, Heart Break Ridge. In the movie former Defensive End for the Cincinnati Bengals, Peter Koch played a marine named The Swede.

In recent years, a new version of the movie Walking Tall, starred another professional athlete that is becoming quite famous for his movies. His name is Dwayne "The Rock" Johnson. While The Rock did not play Buford Pusser in this version of the movie, he was a professional wrestler like Pusser. Also like Pusser, he came from a football background. "The Rock" played defensive end for the University of Miami. The Rock is famous for many action movies, such as The Scorpion King.

There are many athletes that have received such roles for their athletic appearance and physical strength that often accompanies it. Ted Cassidy has been a supporting actor in many movies. At 6'9", and a muscular build, this former Stetson University basketball player is best known for the role of "Lurch" in the "Adams Family" TV series. We remember Ralph Moeller, as a Cyborg, a supporting role in the Gladiator, as well as the starring role in the TV series version of Conan the Barbarian. At nearly 6'6 and nearly 300 lbs., this world class body builder was built in the same mold as David Prowse, making him very marketable in movies requiring a large athletic character. Another athlete with similar body dimensions is John Matuszak. A lineman in the NFL, John is probably best known for his role as Sloth, in the movie "The Goonies". Another 6'8" professional football player receiving similar roles was Ben Davidson. Playing for the raiders during the 1960s, he is probably best known as Rexor, in Conan, The Barbarian, but has also played in movies such as Necessary Roughness, which co-starred several other former football players. Merlin Olson was another large football player who originally became popular in supporting roles that required a large strong man. He later became a supporting actor in the TV drama, "Little House on the Prairie". Of course, we can all remember in Police Academy, when Bubba Smith pulled the seat out of an economy car, so he could drive while sitting in the rear seat. If you ever wondered who the large blonde haired man was in James Bond's Diamonds are Forever, that was Joe Robinson, a British professional wrestler and body builder. In the re-make of The Longest Yard several large athletes were recruited such as wrestlers Kevin Nash, Bill Goldberg, Steve Austin, Bob Sapp and Dalip Singh Rana (The Great Khali), and professional football players Terry Crews, Brian Bosworth, and Michael Irvin. Former FSU full-back Burt Reynolds played two different roles in each of the two versions of this movie. In the 1974 movie he played with several professional football players, including Mike Henry, Ray Nitschke, Jim Nicholson, Pervis Atkins, Joe Kapp and Ernie Wheelwright.

In the movies, the villain is usually the best athlete. This is because they have to be good stuntmen. For example, Clayton Moore, before becoming the ultimate good guy, as the Lone Ranger, began his career, playing villains in old westerns, because he was such a great athlete. The villain was the one that had to fall off his horse, or off a cliff. In the Tarzan movies, the villains were often great athletes. While Gordon Scott was a body builder and a great athlete, some of the villains in the movies where he played Tarzan included Sean Connery, who later turned down the role as Tarzan, and Jock Mahoney who took the role, after Sean turned it down. After Jock Mahoney stopped playing the role, the next Tarzan role paired off an interesting couple. Former football great Mike Henry played Tarzan, while the villain was played by Olympic decathlon gold medalist Rafer Johnson. While Henry was a great athlete; Johnson was considered the greatest athlete of his time.

Many large, athletic men are often cast as villains in movies for other reasons, as well. Given their size, they often have deep, raspy voices that get them type-casted as villains. In many video games, the voices we often hear, without seeing their face belong to actors like former Northwestern University track athlete Clancy Brown (IMDb.com, 2013). We often never recognize some of these guys, until we read the credits at the end of the movie. In the case of David Prowse, another situation presented itself. While he played the role of Darth Vader in Star Wars, he not only wore a mask and a cape, and had to know all of the movie scenes; another man's voice was dubbed over his voice. Mr. Prowse could have walked on the set of Star Wars and not been recognized by people that did not know him. It's like the professional wrestler who said he gets to wear a mask while he is beating someone in the ring, and being ridiculed by fans, then going out for a drink with all of them, later that evening.

Congress is not the only venue where we find wrestlers. We have already mentioned Hulk Hogan, who has starred in many movie roles and currently hosts more than one TV show. Another wrestler-turned-actor is also a politician, serving a term as the governor of Minnesota. This, of course, is Jesse "The Body" Ventura. John "Bradshaw" Layfield played professional football before becoming a professional wrestler. Today, he is a financial advisor on the Fox Business Network. Randy "Macho-Man Savage was a professional baseball player before he became a professional wrestler. Since that time, he has appeared in several movies and TV shows. Several other wrestlers that have been named in this book are Mark Callaway (The Undertaker), Olympic basketball player, wrestler and movie character, El Egante, Dwayne "The Rock" Johnson, George Stults, and Kirk Douglas. Stults had wrestled for the University of Southern Colorado before transferring to Whittier College during his third year to live with his brother Geoff, who played football there. They almost immediately, began playing roles as brothers on the TV series, Seventh Heaven. Former western star John Payne wrestled to work his way through college at Columbia University, during the early 1930s. Another Columbia University wrestler named Nat Pendleton, was a silver medalist in the 1920 Olympics before wrestling professionally and becoming a movie star (briansdriveintheater.com). Woody Strode was a professional wrestler for several years, during the 1950s, before becoming famous for playing villains in many action movies.

An interesting story about two high school teammates occurred when the movie Zookeeper was being advertised in 2011. Former WWE wrestler Mike Foley and Zookeeper star Kevin James were wrestling teammates in high school, in New Jersey. A national news program was showing their photos, as they stood next to each other on their high school wrestling team. Mike jokingly said that he would not let his children see the movie because Kevin had became the most famous member of his high school, instead of him.

In studies where muscle fiber types are examined, a biopsy from the quadriceps muscles illustrated that Olympic wrestlers have more fast-twitch oxidative muscle fiber than any other type of athlete. This is probably because a wrestler is required to compete with a high level of intensity for two minutes without a rest. While other events may last two minutes, the athlete has the opportunity to move away from their opponent or simply slow down, periodically. However, when a wrestler slows down, his opponent will immediately, take advantage of the situation. For this reason, a wrestler must possess more muscle fibers that allow them to perform repeated powerful moves. They must also maintain an attitude of patiently maintaining an intensity that matches each opponent, and wait for their opportunity to use their opponent's mistakes against them and win the match.

A sport that is similar to wrestling is judo. This is one of five sports in which actor Bo Svenson excelled. Like former Senator Ben Campbell, and Russian Prime Minister Putin, Bo wore "the heavy ghee" and threw from a height that would be a bit more painful for their opponent. At over 6'6", Bo Svenson was perhaps one of the five tallest leading men in Hollywood during the 1970s. While we have described several tall athletes who played villains in the movies, few of them were leading men. However, during the 1950s, 60s and 70s, although Chuck Connors was one of our favorite TV western heroes, he often played villains in the movies. In one of these movies, Chuck had a duel with the leading man, played by former UC-Berkley crew athlete, Gregory Peck, in the movie The Big Country. During the 1980s another Swedish-born athlete became a leading man in the movies after making his debut as a villain. This was the two-time European martial arts champion named Dolph Lundgren. After playing a villain in Rocky IV, he played several leading roles such as I Come in Peace, and He-Man. Lundgren was also around 6'6" and shares similar physical features with Svenson. Another martial arts athlete who has played in many action movies is Marc Singer. Most popular for his role as "The Beastmaster", Marc moves like someone who also comes from a track and field background. In the TV game show, entitled, Battle of the Network Stars, Marc passed everyone during the relay race. Although, the teams from the other networks had a tremendous lead, Marc ran like an Olympic track athlete, passing everyone, to win the event.

Several soccer players have become successful in other areas. Most anyone has seen David Beckum in different areas of the media. This guy is so famous that movies are made about him. Other professional soccer players include Andrew Shue (Melrose Place), Eric Cantona (Elizabeth), Robin Williams (Mork and Mindy) and rock singer, Rod Stewart. According to IMDb.com, Robin Williams played soccer for Claremont Men's College. He reportedly wrestled in high school, as well. After playing soccer for Dartmouth College, Andrew Shue played professional soccer before and after becoming a TV star. Like fellow soap star Andrew Shue, Eric Braeden (The Young and the Restless) was a great soccer player before and after becoming a TV star. Jim "Soni" Sonefeld (Drummer for Hootie and the Blowfish) played midfield for the University of South Carolina. The lead singer for his band (Darius Rucker) is also considered one of the best golfers in pop music. Of course, this is based on my former students who were golfers and met

Darius. Another midfielder named John Tesh has been a famous musician as well as a talk show host. Many people from Poland also know a tough young goalie that later became Pope John Paul, who was also well known as perhaps the greatest golfer to ever be a Pope. The rock band, Hootie and the Blowfish includes a college soccer player and a great golfer. Pope John Paul was also well known for both sports. I have heard at least one comedian that made jokes on how the new pope compares to John Paul, as a golfer. Billy Graham is also known for his golf game. He used to be the golf partner of movie star Randolph Scott.

Some of the great stunts performed by many actors make us wonder how may of them were gymnasts. Some of the gymnasts include Patrick Swayze, Chuck Norris, University of Massachusetts gymnast, Richard Gere, and Halley Berry, who most performed most of her own stunts in X-men 3. Frank Merrill, who played Tarzan during the 1920s, was the national gymnastics champion before doing the stunts as Tarzan.

A group of athletes that may be discussed separately include the hosts of news shows and documentaries. We have already mentioned several of these individuals. Jack Hanna (Animal Planet) and Dean Cain (Ripley' Believe It Or Not) were college football players. Bill O'Reilly, host of the O'Reilly Factor, played quarterback and kicker, for the Marist College football team, as well as pitcher for the New York Monarchs semi-pro baseball team. Brian Kilmeade, co-host of Fox and Friends, played soccer for C.W. Post College. Adam Housley, a colleague of O'Reilly and Brian Kilmeade, on Fox News Saturday, played minor league baseball, for the Brewers, and another Fox reporter and co-host of The Five, Eric Bolling played professional baseball for the Pirates. Another co-host of The Five, Bob Beckel played linebacker for Wagner College. He has been quoted concerning his view of quarterbacks, the position he often tackled. Jon Tesh was a midfield soccer player for North Carolina State University, Geraldo Rivera played lacrosse at the University of Arizona and was on the crew team at Maritime college in New York. Anderson Cooper coxed for the Yale crew team, and David Hartman was offered baseball scholarships as well as pro contracts before attending Duke University. As mentioned earlier in this chapter, athlete's careers have been detoured to many reasons. In the case of David Hartman, he was recruited by colleges as well as professional baseball franchises. However, he turned them all down in order to attend Duke University, a very expensive university to attend without a scholarship. However, another news anchor named Bill Hemmer, who loved to play football, chose not to play college football because of the expense of playing ball for a Division III team. This division of college football does not offer scholarships and the tuition at these universities are usually more expensive. Therefore, the Cincinnati native attended Miami of Ohio University, without a football scholarship. There are several athletes mentioned in this book who had similar experiences when they lost their athletic scholarships and had to return to their home states to finish college. In some cases, they may have left the more expensive university where they had an athletic scholarship, in their home state, to finish college at a university with lower tuition. One example we discussed was Fess Parker who played football for HSU, in Texas. However, after his injury, he transferred to the University of Texas where in-state tuition used to be quite low.

Some of the ladies who are news anchors include Robin Roberts, who co-anchored Good Morning America after David Hartman left the show. Roberts played basketball for Southeastern Louisiana University during the 1980s. CNN Anchor, Erin Burnett, played lacrosse and field hockey for Williams College in Massachusetts. Professional tennis champion Cathy Lee Crosby was also a news and sportscaster, former UNC swimmer Laurie Dhue was a Fox News reporter, and former Boston College softball player Elisabeth Hasselbeck co-hosts Fox and Friends.

Two sportscasters have recently attained "rock star" status. Kurt Herbstreet, the former Ohio State University quarterback player, married to one of the OSU cheerleaders, and Lee Corso, a former FSU football player (teammate and friend to Burt Reynolds), and former football coach. Corso is also a unique businessman. He sells the pencils we all used to take the SAT. We have already mention the great sportscaster, Marty Glickman who had to wait until 1998 to receive his award for the gold medal his should have won as a sprinter in the 1936 Olympics.

A group of athletes that must also be considered are martial arts athletes. We have mentioned some of them in other sections of this chapter. Perhaps, the most famous would be Chuck Norris, a six time world kick boxing champion, Chuck has become an icon of our culture. After making several multi-million dollar movies, he now has his own TV show called Walker, Texas Ranger. He has paved the way for many other martial arts athletes. We have already discussed the two time super-heavyweight European Kick Boxing champion, Dolph Lundgren. Many other kick boxing champions have been actors as well. Other members of this club include Jackie Chan and Marc Singer. However, the most recent addition to this list of martial arts athletes is UFC and Mixed Martial Arts champion Quinton 'Rampage' Jackson, the light-heavy champion who is best known as B.A. Baracus in 2010 movie The A-Team where he co-starred with fellow athletes Bradley Cooper and Liam Neeson.

Athletes in other sports include Simon LeBon (Duran Duran) who is a world class yacht racer. He was good enough to perform in the 1988 Olympic Trials, in his home country of England. Like actress Geena Davis, he was already a pop icon in 1988. Yacht racing is another sport in which Bo Svenson excelled. Svenson and LeBon are also accomplished auto racers. Auto racing, America's top sport, includes many celebrities as well. Over the years, we have seen Steve McQueen, James Garner, and Paul Newman, racing cars. Perhaps our most recent addition to this list is Patrick

Dempsey. Robert Stack (The Untouchables) was a champion skeet marksman. Sonja Henie was a gold medalist in ice skating during the 1932 and 1936 Olympics while starring in movies. In Sun Valley Serenade, she co-starred with fellow athlete John Payne.

We could add a category to this chapter. Many of these entertainers were famous as athletes after becoming famous entertainers. As mentioned in the previous paragraph, Simon LeBon was a world class yacht racer after becoming a rock star. Geena Davis made many movies before competing in the 2000 Olympic Trials in archery. Mickey Rourke became a professional boxer after he had become a movie star. Tom Selleck played in senior men's volleyball championships while playing the starring role of one of the top TV series of the 1980s. Like Selleck, Eric Braden had been a champion soccer player after becoming one of the stars of TV's Rat Patrol. Graduating from Dartmouth in 1989, Andrew Shue was an All-American soccer player who played professional soccer before and after starring on the soap opera, "Melrose Place". Ben Johnson was a professional rodeo champion, then a movie star, then a professional rodeo champion, and then a movie star, again. Likewise, Kurt Russell was a teen age movie star when he became a professional baseball player, and returned to the movies after an injury ended his baseball career. Eleanor Holms Jarrett was a famous actress when she took the trip to Germany to defend her record in the back stroke. James Garner owned an auto racing team, during the late 1960s, after becoming a famous movie star. He was also one of the best golfers in Hollywood during this time. After winning the gold medal and breaking the world record in the decathlon, Glen Morris played in one Tarzan movie and then became a professional football player for one season.

Newcomers to the list of athletes who were in the movies before they were college and professional athletes include Patrick Dempsey, who has become a competitive auto racer. Others can be found in starring roles in the 2008 movie The Express.

Rob Brown had been an actor since he was a teen before playing college football for Amherst College, graduating with a degree in psychology shortly before starring in The Express (Wikipedia.org, 2013). Another starring role in this movie went to Geoff Stults, who during the mid 1990s, had played in the TV series Seventh Heaven, around the time he was playing football for Whittier College, in California (where President Nixon played football). Afterward, he played wide receiver for a pro team in Europe (Wikipedia.org, 2013).

While there was no attempt to exclude women from this book, most of these celebrities were athletes during a time when there was little participation available for the ladies. However, there are many impressive ladies that serve in congress, as well as entertainment. We have mentioned Laurie Dhue, Ester Williams, Eleanor Holms Jarrett, Reba McIntyre and Halley Berry. There are many others. While Cathy Lee Crosby is best known as a broadcaster, she was also a well known champion professional tennis player and a TV and movie star. Former undefeated boxing champ Laila Ali has been a co-host of the American Gladiators. She has other relations to sport as well. Other than being the daughter of boxing champ Mohammed Ali, her husband is former NFL receiver Curtis Conway. Geena Davis became a world class athlete while she was making movies. She was in the 2000 Olympic trials in archery. Perhaps the most alarming story among females is that of Eleanor Holms Jarrett. As the women's champion in the backstroke, and a well-known actress, she was returning to defend her title in the 1936 Olympics, when she was kicked off the team after rumors that she trained on champagne and caviar. Many years later, she was interviewed during the Olympics and she jokingly said that he still likes champagne. Although, she did not get to compete in the 1936 Olympics, she co-starred in a Tarzan movie, immediately after the Games, with the 1936 Olympic Decathlon champion, and world record holder, Glen Morris. As mentioned earlier, an Olympic champion from the 1932 and 1936 Olympics was 1930s and 40s movie star Sonja Henie. Most of the women we could mention are young women that have recently became famous entertainers such as Laurie Dhue from the Fox News network. However, another young softball player from Boston College named Elisabeth Hasselbeck. She was the co-host of a popular show called The View and currently is a co-host of Fox and Friends. As an athlete with a reputable work ethic, it is not surprising she is married to NFL quarterback, Tim Hasselbeck.

It is not surprising that so many movies about comic book characters have given the starring roles to former athletes. Dean Cain as Superman, Reb Brown as Captain America, Matthew Fox as Racer X, the many actors who played in Tarzan movies, and the many actors who played in Xmen movies. One of these Xmen is currently becoming one of the up-and-coming stars of the decade. Taylor Kitsch played the role of Gambit in Xmen Origins: Wolverine. A former hockey player for the BCHL team, Langley Hornets, during his 20s, he was mostly known for his role as Tim Riggins, in 68 episodes of Friday Night Lights (Wikipedia.org, 2013). At the age of 30, he is highly demanded as a model 2012 movie starring roles such as John Carter and Battleship, as well as a new Xmen movie. In his free time he uses his athletic abilities in sports such as triathlons to fund charities. Although there are still several athletes in these action movies, because of the technology in action movies, the percent of athletes in these movies is actually much smaller. The older action heroes had to do so many of their own stunts that they had to be athletes.

Celebrity golf has always been important in Hollywood. In the December 2005 issue of Golf Digest a list of entertainers were listed with their golf handicaps. The list of actors with no more than an eight (breaking the score of 80) would include Samuel L. Jackson, Chris O'Donnell, Kevin Sorbo, Kurt Russell, Matthew McConaughey, Bill Murray, Hugh Grant, Craig T. Nelson, and

Randy Quaid. Of course, this list was led by Randy Quaid's younger brother Dennis, with a handicap of "one". A country artist named Vince Gill also has a handicap of "one". However, the long-standing Hollywood champion, Jack Wagner had not played very much that year, and went out and broke 'par", as he had repeatedly done in the past. This is not a surprise, considering Jack was the Missouri State Junior College Champion in 1980, before transferring to the University of Arizona (People, December 17, 1984). Some of the younger entertainers that may give these guys a tough game include country music star Kip Moore, who grew up in Tifton, Georgia, near Callaway Gardens. His father was a golf pro, and Kip landed a golf scholarship with Valdosta State University, but turned to music as a career (Sliva, About.com). According to Fabian (About.com), country music star, Jake Owen is one of the many athletes who was on his way to a pro career as an FSU golfer when an injury ended his golf career, and he began learning to be a musician while he was injured.

According to Jerry Tarde, the editor-in-chief for Golf Digest listed the top five all-time Hollywood golfers, according to their ability (December, 2005). These entertainers were Bing Crosby, Bob Hope, Bob Sterling, Katharine Hepburn, and James Garner. James Garner is also mentioned in this book as a race car driver, and Bob Hope was a professional boxer.

Celebrities are constantly competing in sport, for charity events, as well as televised competitions between entertainers. Teams often seek out the athletes that can perform for their TV series or TV station. Several movies also portray sport. They always need former athletes to play in them. This is usually not a problem, considering the large number of athletes becoming actors. Several of the athletes in this book competed in more than one sport. Usually, I can pick out the members of a cast who were college, Olympic or professional athletes. As stated throughout throughout this book, "athletic grace" is difficult to fake. However, the percent of athletes used in action movies is decreasing. In older movies, so many of the stunts had to be performed by the actor that athletes were needed for the role. Today, new technology has replaced some of this need.

This information could also be useful in the following chapters. How many of your favorite entertainers can you indentify as athletes? What was their sport(s) in college? Was your congressman an athlete? Did your favorite entertainer play ball against your congressman?

The following chapters will give the reader a chance to see how many different ways these athletes can be compared. These quizzes include actors, and musicians, and members of our government. How many of the actors in Field of Dreams caught a baseball, without having to go through training, first? How many actors in action movies needed a stuntman for most of the performances? How many actors in a movie were teammates, or competed against each other in college or professional sport? How many college and professional athletes played in movies together? How many congressmen competed against each other in college? See how many of your favorite entertainers competed with each other or with your congressman. See how many of your favorite entertainers played ball against my congressman. These chapters should reveal some of your favorite celebrities in ways that may surprise you. I hope you enjoy this trivia.

CHAPTER 4

QUIZZES CONCERNING POLITICIANS AND CELEBRITIES WHO WERE ATHLETES

(See chapter 5 for the answers to the following questions and quizzes)

Which of the celebrities named in this book were college or professional baseball players?

Which of the celebrities named in this book played college or professional basketball?

Which of the politicians named in this book played college or professional football?

Which of the entertainers named in this book played college (not professional) football?

Which of the entertainers named in this book played professional or semi-pro football?

Which of the celebrities named in this book were college and/or Olympic Swimmers?

Which of the celebrities named in this book played college or professional soccer, hockey, or lacrosse?

Which of the celebrities named in this book was college or professional boxers (or military champions)?

Which of the celebrities named in this book was college, Olympic or professional martial arts athletes?

Which of the celebrities named in this book were college or professional wrestlers?

Which of the celebrities named in this book was college, Olympic or national champion track athletes?

Which of the celebrities named in this book were college or professional rodeo cowboys?

Which of the celebrities named in this book competed in more than one college or professional sport?

Which of the celebrities named in this book have either competed in the Olympics or Olympic Trails?

Athletes who were teammates or competed in sports against each other.

1. The Congressman known as the world's greatest athlete competed against Gunsmoke's Chester during the 1948 Olympic Trials.

2. Patrick Star may have played football against a congressman.

3. The duck hunter's backup quarterback played in the NFL against a congressman.

4. During the 1990s, one of the Expendables played in the NFL against a congressman.

5. Before WWII ended their sports careers The Range Rider would have played basketball against a senator and presidential candidate.

6. Although, congressmen and senators often disagree, two of them were basketball teammates when they played for the Knicks.

7. During the early 1970s, two LA Rams coaches had sons playing quarterback in college who would have been teammates at UCLA if one of the coaches had not taken the position coaching the Redskins and his son transferred to UVA. One of the quarterbacks became a movie star and one became a governor as and senator.

8. Hunter had the job of sacking a New York senator when they both played in the NFL.

9. Who was that senator from Virginia that was beaten by the Annapolis boxing champion?

10. Congressmen had to play basketball against each other where one was from Georgia and one from Tennessee.

11. Hercules would have played basketball against a senator if one of them had not left the Midwest to play for BIOLA in California.

12. This is the story of two quarterbacks from Louisiana Tech University. Both were offered NFL contracts, but one went home to go duck hunting.

13. Although, the congressman was a good quarterback at Harvard, it's still tough to get the ball past an All-American safety who is a superman.

14. The MVP in the 1926 Rose Bowl tuned down professional football to be a movie star, while the guy trying to tackle him, made a stop at the Olympics before becoming a movie star as well.

15. Before playing in the NFL and boxing professionally, Magnum's roommate and Captain America were teammates at USC.

16. When the duck hunter went home to Louisiana, Al Bundy kept his teammate company in Pittsburg.

17. The Quiet Man and his priest were teammates at USC.

18. The 1960 Gold Medalist competed against the top football player during the 1955 National Decathlon Championship.

19. Other than competing in the 1955 decathlon champions, Jim also played pro football against two guys who would later play in the movie The Undefeated with a few other former athletes.

20. Don't get confused between a basketball player from USC who became a famous actor and one from CSULA who

became a famous pop singer just because they are tall, with dark hair, and a mustache and played ball for universities in the same city near the same time. One of them did not begin playing ball until the other graduated.

21. They would have been teammates at Columbia if they were closer in age.

22. They would have been teammates for the Buffalo Bills, except for their knee injuries.

23. Superman played college football against Lost Jack.

24. An All-American half-back turned western movie star played against Tarzan in the 1926 Rose Bowl.

25. Hunter and Apollo Creed were teammates at San Diego State University.

26. Hunter and Flash Gordon were teammates in the NFL.

27. A Heisman nominee from Cornell would have played against the General from The Rock in Ivy League football.

28. Al Bundy went to NFL training camp with the duck stalker's backup quarterback.

29. Two USC football teammates played roles in The Quiet Man.

30. Before they each played the role of Tarzan, they were teammates during the Olympics.

31. Although, the two biggest country singers played positions in football where they would have lined up across from each other, it would not be allowed.

32. Three football players at Columbia University from different generations have each played characters in science fiction movies.

33. Two crew athletes at Yale who are famous for playing monsters in the movies.

34. Two Olympic athletes who were removed from the 1936 Olympic team for questionable reasons.

35. Two young country singers from the NCAA Division I universities in the south who probably competed against each other in golf.

36. Congressman A and NFL football player and a TV psychologist would have been teammates during the early 1970s if the TV psychologist had not been injured and transferred to a university near his home in Texas.

37. Two athletes on the 1936 Olympic team who played in a Tarzan movie together.

38. Many movie stars are former professional wrestlers.

39. A U. S. vice president and a movie star and college athlete threw the discus at a high school known for educating the children of politicians.

40. The young Harvard QB and future congressman also worked summers for a senator who had been an athlete for the rival team, coached by a U. S. president.

41. An Arkansas senator played college football against an Oklahoma congressman and NFL football player.

42. A Kansas congressman and Kim Kardasian's stepfather were teammates on the 1972 Olympic track team, while a Maryland congressman and his teammates turned down their silver medal in basketball.

43. The Kansas congressman named in the previous statement was also in 1964 Olympics with two U. S. senators, one of which played pro ball with the Maryland congressman.

44. A Pennsylvania congressman played football against Captain America and that tough guy that played in so many action movies, and the NFL.

45. Several professional basketball players are named in this book.

46. An Oklahoma Congressman and one of the members of Robin Hood's band of merry men played Canadian Football and are about the same age.

47. An Olympic and Professional Basketball player who became a senator shared a locker room with a three sport athlete at who became a congressman.

Athletes who played in movies together.

1. A UCLA quarterback played in the villain in Crossfire Trail in which the leading man was a USC basketball player. This UCLA quarterback also played the sheriff, in another western in which the Role of Wyatt Earp was played by a CSU-Fullerton baseball player, and his younger brother Warren was played by a former college basketball player.

2. The CSU-Fullerton baseball player, named in the previous statement, starred in Field of Dreams with a circus performer who had previously played the role of Wyatt Earp in which the role of Doc Holliday was played by a college wrestler.

3. The wrestler named in the previous statement, co-starred in The War Wagon with a USC football player, and played the villain in the movie named The Villain, with Mr. Olympia.

4. The USC football player named in the previous question, starred in movies with several other athletes, including, at least one of the actors who played in Tarzan movies. He's also well-known for starring in several movies, such as "The Searchers" and "The Quiet Man", with his teammate from USC, who played in several other movies, such as "Gone With The Wind", and was the star of the TV series, Wagon Train.

5. One of the actors named in the previous statement, not only played Tarzan, with co-stars, such as the 1960 Olympic decathlon champion, he also played in other movies, co-starring his fellow athletes. Two of these movies, "The

Longest Yard" and "Smokey and The Bandit," starred a football player from FSU.

6. One of the actors that played the villain in Tarzan movies, also played in another movie with the 1960 Olympic decathlon champion, and was a college decathlete, as well, before playing professional football for the Rams, then becoming a professional wrestler before co-starring in roles such as Spartacus with the former wrestler named in the second statement on this page.

7. The FSU football player playing in Smokey and the Bandit has played in many roles, with many other former athletes, other than the man named in the previous question. He also played in "Smokey and the Bandit II with one of the greatest NFL quarterbacks, an NFL linebacker who played in Tarzan movies, and the daughter of another famous athlete who played Tarzan, in the movies.

8. Before playing the role of Tarzan, in the 1960s, an athlete mentioned in the previous statement first starred in a TV series called Range Rider, which was produced by a former baseball player, who became The Singing Cowboy, producing many TV series and buying his own baseball team. As one of the greatest stuntmen in Hollywood, before playing this role, he played the villain in a movie series with a former Dartmouth football player.

9. One of the first TV westerns series starred a former circus performer who began his acting career playing villains in westerns starring the Singing Cowboy and MBL team owner, named in the previous statement.

10. A few rodeo cowboys played co-starring roles with John Wayne in movies such as Chism, The Undefeated, McClintock, and The Searchers.

11. A 260 pound martial arts champion killed an NFL football player in Rocky IV.

12. Two of Ben Cartwright's sons as well as his top ranch-hand were college athletes.

13. The Range Rider was a three sport college athlete and his side-kick was a rodeo cowboy.

14. In The Crimson Pirate, two former partners in the circus co-starred in the movie.

15. A crew athlete had to fight a pro baseball and basketball player in The Big Country.

16. Because of their athletic abilities and the lack of a blue screen, many of the athletes in westerns played in movies with each other during the 1940s, 50s and 60s. We have mentioned some of them. However, we can probably make a separate list of TV western stars that played in each other's shows and they were also in movies together.

17. Two college football players played in westerns together during the 1940s and 50s. One of them retired and one was beginning his career as the best stuntman in Hollywood before he was Tarzan.

18. A professional boxer co-starred with a college baseball player in City Slickers.

19. Several TV shows include multiple athletes on their show such as a water polo player who stars on Hope and Faith when one of the female characters was dating an All-American football player from Princeton who also played Volleyball. One of the last times O. J. Simpson was on a TV show was when he played a part on In the Heat of the Night, which starred another profession football player. In the episode, O. J. Simpson's character had played college football for Mississippi, against one of the stars of the show whose character played football for Alabama.

Athletes-turn-actor who played the same roles

1. The role of Wyatt Earp has been played by many actors. However, this role is probably best known, by the current generation through two baseball players, one circus performer, and a race car driver.

2. The role of Doc Holliday has also been played by athletes. A wrestler played the role with the circus performer, and one of the best golfers in Hollywood played the role with the CSU-Fullerton baseball player.

3. This book lists several athletes who have played the role of Tarzan. Three were known to be swimmers, two were Olympic track athletes, six played college or professional football players, two played college basketball, one gymnast and one was bodybuilder.

4. The role of Roman Brady on the soap opera, "Days of our Lives" has been played by a baseball player for the Yankees, and a Dartmouth College quarterback.

5. Flash Gordon was originally played by an Olympic swimmer. Forty years later, the role would star a receiver for the Rams.

6. In parts two and three of the original "Walking Tall" trilogy, a multi-sport athlete shared a military past with the character in which the movie was based. Although, the 21st century version of "Walking Tall," was not based on the true-story of Buford Pusser, the role was played by another professional wrestler (like Pusser). Another movie called Walking Tall, starred a four sport college athlete mentioned, repeatedly in this book.

7. The role of Frankenstein has obviously been played by large athletes. In England this character was played by the same 6'7" body builder who later played Darth Vader, in "Star Wars." Several years later, a discus thrower from Northwestern University would play the role, in "The Bride."

8. In Conan the Barbarian, Mr. Olympia became a house-hold name. In the TV series, perhaps the largest body builder since David Prowse played the role after being a Cyborg, and before co-starring in Gladiator.

9. The role of Hercules has been played by many athletes. However, this generation would probably best remember three body builders, one of whom was also a professional football player who played the role in the movies. A four sport college athlete from Moorehead State University (now MSU, Moorehead) made the character famous in the 1990s TV series and movies.

10. One of the athletes who played Hercules also played the role of Kull the Conqueror, which was also played by a

multi-sport athlete who is best known for his role in the 1960s TV series, Laredo.

11. The best known actors to play the role of Davey Crockett were played by two college football players. One played for Hardin-Simmons University, in Texas, and the other played for the University of Southern California. However, a heavy-weight boxer from Montana also played the role.

12. While they did not play the same character, the two major side-kicks for Matt Dillon, in the long running series, Gunsmoke, were played by an All-American decathlete from Oklahoma, and a rodeo cowboy, who had previously played in The Searchers with the USC football player named in the previous statement. When neither of them was in the show, Marshall Dillon teamed up with an FSU football player known for his roles in Smokey and the Bandit and The Longest Yard.

13. Several former college and professional football players played various roles in the two versions of The Longest Yard.

14. A football player for Hardin-Simmons University played Daniel Boone on TV, long after a navy boxing champion played the role in the movies.

Athletes who played athletes in the movies.

1. A former USC basketball player played the role of President Eisenhower.

2. A former circus performer played the role of Jim Thorpe, as well as Dr. Archie "Moonlight" Graham.

3. A two-time Olympic decathlon champion, college football player, and congressman, played himself in a movie about himself.

4. A California governor and champion body builder played the role of famous body builder Hargity, whose wife (Jane Mansfield), and daughter, were famous actors.

5. A famous football player with the Chicago Bears played the role of Babe Zaharias' husband, who was a famous professional wrestler.

6. A former Michigan State University football player and Rodeo Cowboy played the role of Chicago Bears full-back, Brian Piccolo.

7. A former Columbia University wide receiver played the role of Marshall University Coach Red Dawson.

8. A former college basketball player played the role of golf legend Bobby Jones.

9. A former Florida State University football player played the role of Coach Bear Bryant in Forest Gump.

10. What famous TV star, famous for having been a great high school football player, who becomes a shoe salesman with America's most dysfunctional family, was really a great college football player, and good enough to go to training camp with the Steelers, landing him in more than one role as a coach?

11. The 1976 Olympic decathlon champion played the role of John Capelletti, before he was Kim Kardasian's step father.

12. The former manager of the University of Tennessee played the role of a decathlete going to the 1980 Olympics, in The Golden Moment.

13. A five sport athlete played the role of former pro wrestler and Tennessee sheriff Buford Pusser.

14. The Harvard University football player known for his riding abilities played the role of Ty Cobb.

15. A former professional baseball player played the role of the U.S. Olympic Hockey coach in Miracle.

16. A CSU baseball player has played in roles as a cyclist, a golfer, and a few baseball movies.

17. A former USC football player played the role of Bob Mathias' high school track coach in the Bob Mathias Story.

18. A former college swimmer and football player played the role of a professional baseball player as well as a college football player before becoming President of the USA.

19. One of the greatest golfers in Hollywood not only played the role of MLB player Jimmy Morris, but also more than one role as a professional football player.

20. There are many movies made about sport and many athletes have been needed to play roles in these movies.

Who's in the News

1. Three professional baseball players on Fox News.

2. A college softball player on Fox News whose husband and brother-in-law are NFL quarterbacks.

3. A college soccer player does the sports on Fox News.

4. Of course, the big guy on The Five played linebacker in college.

5. The guy that gives the 9:00 am news on Fox thought playing football at a Division III college would be too expensive.

6. A UNC swimmer who use to be on Fox News.

7. On Ohio football player from Tennessee give the news about animals.

8. The Hulk's crew teammate at Yale is a news anchor for CNN.

9. The pretty lady on CNN played lacrosse and field hockey for Williams College.

10. After a baseball player left Good Morning America, his replacement was a lady basketball player from Southeastern Louisiana State University.

11. The entertainment news was given by a soccer playing musician from NCSU.

12. President Obama's first press secretary played soccer for NCSU.

13. How many sportscasters should we name?

CHAPTER 5

ANSWERS TO QUIZ QUESTIONS IN CHAPTER FOUR

The following celebrities were college or professional baseball players.

x_____ President Dwight Eisenhower

x_____ President George W. Bush

x_____ President George H. W. Bush

x_____ Senator Zell Miller

x_____ Senator Pete Domenici

x_____ Senator Jim Bunning

x_____ Kurt Russell

x_____ Chuck Connors

x_____ Drake Hogestyn

x_____ Tim McGraw

x_____ Kevin Costner

x_____ Billy Ray Cyrus

x_____ Billy Crystal

x_____ Bill O'Reilly

x_____ Governor Haley Barbour

x_____ Charley Pride

x_____ Roy Acuff

x_____ Bob Uecker

x_____ Anderson Davis

x_____ Brad Johnson

The following celebrities played college or professional basketball.

x_____ Senator Bob Dole

x_____ Senator Bill Bradley

x_____ Congressman Tom McMillen

x_____ Congressman Ander Crenshaw

x_____ Congressman Bob Ethridge

x_____ Congressman John Tanner

x_____ Congressman Henry Hyde

x_____ Congressman Baron Hill

x_____ Congressman Tom Osborne

x_____ Congressman Scotty Baesler

x_____ Congressman Tom McMillen

x_____ Paul Wight

x_____ Chuck Connors

x_____ Chuck Negron

x_____ Denny Miller

x_____ Kevin Sorbo

x_____Jock Mahoney

x_____ Ted Cassidy

x_____ Mark Callaway

x_____ Bob Barker

x_____James Caviezel

x_____ Billy Dean

x_____ Tom Selleck

x_____ Mike Connors (Mannix)

x_____ Bill Cosby

x_____ Shaquille O'Neal

x_____ Marques Johnson

x_____ Tyler Mane

x_____ Marc Blucas

x.____ Wilt Chamberlain

x_____ Rick Fox
x_____ Kareem Abdul Jabar

The following politicians played college or professional football.

x_____ President Ronald Reagan
x_____ President Dwight Eisenhower
x_____ President Gerald Ford
x_____ President John Kennedy
x_____ Senator Jack Kemp
x_____ Senator Bob Dole
x_____ Senator John Edwards
x_____ Senator Edward Kennedy
x_____ Senator William T. Stachowski
x_____ Senator George Allen
x_____ Senator Chuck Hagel
x_____ Congressman J.C. Watts
x_____ Congressman Steve Largent
x_____ Congressman Rick Renzi
x_____ Congressman J.D. Hayworth
x_____ Congressman John Jack Murtha
x_____ Congressman Tim Holden
x_____ Congressman John Boozman
x_____ Congressman Ron Kind
x_____ Congressman Tom Allen
x_____ Congressman Heath Shuler
x_____ Congressman Zackary Space
x_____ Congressman Jason Altmire
x_____ Congressman Tom Osborne
x_____ Congressman Bob Mathias
x_____ Congressman Mike Kelly

The following entertainers were professional or semi-pro football players

x_____ Alan Autry
x_____ Fred Dryer
x_____ Forrest Tucker
x_____ William Smith
x_____ Jim Brown
x_____ Ed Marinaro
x_____ Bernie Casey
x_____ Merlin Olson
x_____ Roman Gabriel
x_____ Sam J. Jones
x_____ Carl Weathers
x_____ Terry Crews
x_____ John Matuszak
x_____ Ben Davidson
x_____ Terry Bradshaw
x_____ Howie Long
x_____ Toby Keith
x_____ D J Lockhart-Johnson
x_____ Glen Morris
x_____ Bubba Smith
x_____ Fred Williamson
x_____ Tim Rossovich
x_____ Mike Reid
x_____ Woody Strode
x_____ Dean Cain
x_____ Eric Alan Kramer
x_____ O. J. Simpson
x_____ Joe Namath

The following entertainers played college football.

x_____ Tommy Lee Jones

x_____ Bill Cosby

x_____ Garth Brooks

x_____ Burt Reynolds

x_____ Matthew Fox

x_____ Robert Urick

x_____ Gary Morris

x_____ Reb Brown

x_____ John Wayne

x_____ Jock Mahoney

x_____ George Lindsey

x_____ Dan Blocker

x_____ Phil McGraw

x_____ Ward Bond

x_____ Miles O'Keefe

x_____ Bill O'Reilly

x_____ David Canary

x_____ Fess Parker

x_____ Mark Harmon

x_____ Ozzie Nelson

x_____ Daniel Cudmore

x_____ Ed Harris

x_____ Trace Adkins

x_____ Jack Hanna

x_____ Johnny Mack Brown

x_____ Randolph Scott

x_____ Sonny Shroyer

x_____ Hugh Beaumont

x_____ Craig Sheffer

x_____ Charles Starrett
x_____ Jack Lord
x_____ John Bolger
x_____ Kris Kristofferson
x_____ Rob Brown
x_____ Geoff Stults
x_____ Jack Palance
x_____ Brad Harris
x_____ Ty Hardin

The following were swimmers, divers, or water polo players

x_____ President Ronald Reagan
x_____ President John Kennedy
x_____ Ted McGinley
x_____ Eleanor Holms Jarrett
x_____ Laurie Dhue
x_____ Johnny Weissmuller
x_____ Buster Crabbe
x_____ Ester Williams
x_____ Jock Mahoney
x_____ Jason Statham
x_____ Viggo Mortensen
x_____ Vince Edwards

The following were lacrosse, hockey, rugby, or soccer players

x_____ President George W. Bush
x_____ Liam Neeson
x_____ John Tesh
x_____ Andrew Shue
x_____ Kevin Sorbo

x_____ Rod Stewart

x_____ Congressman Dutch Ruppersberger

x_____ Geraldo Rivera

x_____ Jim "Soni" Sonefeld

x_____ Jim Brown

x_____ Eric Cantona

x_____ Taylor Kitsch

x_____ Brian Kilmeade

x_____ Erin Burnett

x_____ Robin Williams

The following celebrities were college, military champions, or professional boxers.

x_____ President Teddy Roosevelt

x_____ Senator John McCain

x_____ Senator James Webb

x_____ Colonel Oliver North

x_____ Bob Hope

x_____ Buddy Baer

x_____ Max Baer Jr.

x_____ Tony Danza

x_____ Jack Palance

x_____ Reb Brown

x_____ Robert Conrad

x_____ George Montgomery

x_____ George O'Brien

x_____ Richard Boone

x_____ Dale Robertson

x_____ Micky Rourke

x_____ John Payne

x_____ Kris Kristofferson

x_____ Robert Ryan

The following wrestled in college, the Olympics, or as a professional.

x_____ President Abraham Lincoln
x_____ Senator Paul Wellstone
x_____ Senator Alan Cranston
x_____ Congressman Dennis Hastert
x_____ Congressman Jim Jordan
x_____ Secretary Donald Rumsfeld
x_____ Congressman Jim Leach
x_____ Governor Jesse Ventura
x_____ Dwayne Johnson
x_____ Mark Callaway
x_____ Tyler Mane
x_____ John Payne
x_____ Terry Bollea
x_____ Kevin Nash
x_____ Paul Wight
x_____ Nat Pendleton
x_____ Hillbilly Jim Morris
x_____ Mike Mazurki
x_____ Kirk Douglas

The following were college or world class track athletes

x_____ Senator Bob Dole
x_____ Senator Strom Thurmond
x_____ Congressman Jim Ryun
x_____ Congressman Tom Allen
x_____ Congressman Rob Simmons
x_____ Congressman Tom Osborne

x_____ Congressman Bob Mathias

x_____ Michael Landon

x_____ Garth Brooks

x_____ Dennis Weaver

x_____ Bill Cosby

x_____ Herman Brix

x_____Bo Svenson

x_____ Clancy Brown

x_____ Rosie Greer

x_____ Glen Morris

x_____ Herman Brix

x_____ Bruce Dern

x_____ Bruce Jenner

x_____ Rafer Johnson

x_____ Woody Strode

x_____ O. J. Simpson

The following were Rodeo Cowboys

x_____ Ron White

x_____ James Caan

x_____ Ben Johnson

x_____ Reba McIntire

x_____ Hoot Gibson

x_____ Hank Worden

x_____ Tom Mix

x_____ Ken Curtis

x_____ Brad Johnson

x_____ Toby Keith

x_____ Slim Pickens

x_____ Dick West

The following competed in more than one college or professional sport.

x_____ President Teddy Roosevelt rowed at Harvard and was a professional boxer.

x_____ President Ronald Reagan was a swimmer and a football player at Eureka College.

x_____ President George W. Bush was a baseball player as well as a rugby player at Yale.

x_____ President John Kennedy was a swimmer, golfer and football player at Harvard.

x_____ Senator Bob Dole ran track, and played football and basketball at the University of Kansas.

x_____ Congressman Tom Allen ran track and played football in college.

x_____ Congressman Bob Mathias played football, turning down the Washington Redskins, and ran track at Stanford, winning two gold medals in the Olympic decathlon.

x_____ Congressman Tom Osborne ran track and played football during college.

x_____ Chuck Connors played baseball and basketball during college and professional.

x_____ Jock Mahoney was a swimmer, football and basketball player at Iowa.

x_____ Bill O'Reilly played football and baseball during college and played semi-pro baseball.

x_____ Reb Brown played football for USC and boxed professionally.

x_____ James Caan played football for Michigan State and was a professional rodeo cowboy.

x_____ Mark Callaway played basketball during college and wrestled professionally.

x_____ Dwayne Johnson played football during college and wrestled professionally.

x_____ John Layfield played college and professional football and wrestled professionally.

x_____ Bruce Jenner played college football and ran track, and was an Olympic gold medalist in the decathlon.

x_____ Jim Brown, ran track, played lacrosse and football during college and played professional football.

x_____ Tyler Mane played college basketball and wrestled professionally.

x_____ Kevin Nash played college basketball and wrestled professionally.

x_____ Terry Bradshaw was the national javelin throwing champion during college, and played college and professional football.

x_____ Phil Simms played baseball and football during college and was the MVP in the 1987 Superbowl as the quarterback for the New York Giants.

x_____ Kevin Sorbo played football, basketball, hockey and baseball during college, and is one of the best golfers in Hollywood.

x_____ Dean Cain played football and volleyball at Princeton University.

x_____ Woody Strode was a college decathlete, and football player, and wrestled and played football professionally.

x_____ Bill Cosby played football, basketball and ran track for Temple University.

x_____ Rafer Johnson played basketball and ran track for UCLA and was the 1960 Olympic decathlon champion.

x_____ Herman Brix played football and threw the shot put during college and was a silver medalist in the 1928 Olympics in the shot put.

x____ Rosie Greer threw the discus and played football for Penn State University, and played professional football.

x____ Mike Reid was a wrestler and a football player at Penn State before he played in the NFL for the Cincinnati Bengals.

x____ Paul Wight played basketball at Wichita State University before becoming Big Show in professional wrestling.

x____ Dale Robertson received 32 awards in eight sports during college and boxed professionally.

x____ Glenn Morris won the 1936 Olympic decathlon before playing professional football.

x____ Kris Kristofferson was a football player and a boxer during college.

x____ Geraldo Rivera was a crew athlete at Maritime College and played lacrosse for the University of Arizona.

x____ Jack Palance was a professional boxer who played football for UNC.

x____ Craig Sheffer played football and baseball for ESSU.

x____ Before Brad Johnson was a professional steer wrestler; he played baseball for Oregon State University.

x____ Erin Burnett played lacrosse and field hockey at Williams College.

x____ Joe Robinson was a professional wrestler and a body builder.

x____ Brad Harris was a college football player and a body builder.

x____ O. J. Simpson was a college track athlete and a professional football player.

The following competed in the Olympics or competed in the Olympic Trials.

x_____ Senator Ben Campbell

x_____ General George Patton

x_____ Congressman Bob Mathias

x_____ Congressman Jim Ryun

x_____ Rafer Johnson

x_____ Bruce Jenner

x_____ Johnny Weissmuller

ATHLETES ON THE STUMP AND THE STAGE

x_____ Buster Crabbe
x_____ Eleanor Holms Jarrett
x_____ Herman Brix
x_____ Glen Morris
x_____ Marty Glickman (on the team but was replaced)
x_____ Sonja Henie
x_____ Geena Davis
x_____ Simon Le Bon
x_____ Jason Statham
x_____ Nat Pendleton

The following congressmen and pop stars were either teammates or competed against each other in sport.

1. Most everyone knows that former Congressman Bob Mathias was the two-time Olympic gold medalist in the decathlon. However, when he won the 1948 Olympic trials, sixth place went to a man named Billy D. Weaver, who later became Dennis Weaver, when he became a major movie star. He is probably best known for his TV roles as Chester, in Gunsmoke, and the starring role in McCloud.

2. Congressman Rick Renzi played football for North Arizona University around the same time that TV and movie star Bill Fagerbakke was playing football for the University of Idaho.

3. Congressman Steve Largent was setting reception records for the Seattle Seahawks, when Terry Bradshaw was setting passing records for the Pittsburg Steelers.

4. Congressman Heath Shuler and Terry Crews played against each other in the NFL.

5. Senator Bob Dole played football and basketball at the University of Kansas around the same time that Jock Mahoney played for the University of Iowa (a team that would have played against Kansas).

6. Senator Bill Bradley and Congressman Tom McMillan were teammates playing basketball for the New York Knicks.

7. Senator George Allen and actor Mark Harmon were both quarterbacks for UCLA while their fathers coached for the Rams. However, when Coach Allen took the position with the Washington Redskins, George transferred to the University of Virginia, where he was an All-ACC quarterback, and played against Clemson University where another senator named John Edwards played wide receiver.

8. Senator Jack Kemp and Fred Dryer played football against each other in the NFL.

9. Senator James Webb and Colonel Oliver North boxed against each other at Annapolis.

10. Congressman John Tanner and Congressman Andrew Crenshaw played basketball around the same time, in the SEC, during college.

11. Senator John Thune and Kevin Sorbo were two boys from the Midwest who played college basketball, however, Thune played college ball in California.

12. Terry Bradshaw and Phil Robertson were college football teammates at Louisiana Tech University.

13. Congressman Ron Kind played quarterback for Harvard when Dean Cain played free safety for Princeton, in the same conference.

14. Johnny Mack Brown and Herman Brix played against each other in the 1926 Rose Bowl.

15. Tim Rossovich and Reb Brown were college teammates for one year at USC. Each of them is well known as character actors in action roles. Reb has also been a leading man in movies such as the comic book character Captain America.

16. Ed O'Neil and Terry Bradshaw began playing for the Steelers the same year.

17. John Wayne and Ward Bond were football teammates at USC.

18. Rafer Johnson and Jim Brown competed against each other in the National Championships in the decathlon.

19. Jim Brown, Roman Gabriel, and Merlin Olson played against each other in the NFL.

20. Tom Selleck played basketball at USC while Chuck Negron was playing at CSULA. However, Tom did not begin playing for USC until Chuck graduated.

21. Although they played during different generations, Matthew Fox, Brian Dennehy and Ed Harris each played college football for Columbia University.

22. Burt Reynolds was supposed to play for the Bills during the late 1950s, Forry Smith played during the mid 1970s and Dean Cain played in 1989. A knee injury ended all of their football careers with the Bills. Then they became TV and movie stars. While Reynolds would probably have retired before Smith was drafted, Smith would have still been playing when Cain was drafted.

23. Dean Cain, who played superman in the 1990s, played safety for Princeton during the late 1980s. One of the teams in their conference was Columbia University, where the wide receiver was Matthew Fox, star of many movies, and the popular TV series, Lost.

24. Western movie star Johnny Mack Brown was an All-American half back for Alabama when he was the MVP in the 1926 Rose Bowl. However, the guy playing tackle for the opposing team made many westerns, as well. After winning the silver medal for the shot put in the 1928 Olympics, Herman Brix (Bruce Bennett) became best known for his role as Tarzan, a role he played during the 1930s.

25. Fred Dryer, who is probably best known for his TV series, Hunter, played college football for San Diego State University. One of his teammates was Carl Weathers, who is best known for his role as Apollo Creed, in the Rocky movies. Each of them also played professional football before becoming movie stars.

26. Fred Dryer (Hunter) and Sam J. Jones (Flash Gordon) played for the Rams. Dryer was a defensive end and Jones was a receiver.

27. Ed Marinero was a Heisman nominee at Cornell University before playing in the NFL. Although he has played in many movies, he is probably best known for his role on the TV series called Hill Street Blues. One of the rival schools for Cornell was Columbia University where a future movie star was playing football during the late 1960s, was Ed Harris, the star of many movies such as The Rock, and The Abyss.

28. Ed O'Neill is best known for his TV character, Al Bundy. However, he almost had a career playing football for the Pittsburg Steelers. Although, he did not make the final cut, he was teammates, during training camp with another football player, who made the final cut and went on to become the team's quarterback when they won four Super Bowl Championships. Terry Bradshaw, was also college teammates with Phil Robertson.

29. John Wayne is one of most recognized western movie stars in history. He has made hundreds of movies. Many of these movies co-starred his football teammate from the University of Southern California, Ward Bond, who starred in many movies, without Wayne, including his 1960s TV series, Wagon Train.

30. Johnny Weissmuller and Buster Crabbe were teammates in the 1928 and 1932 Olympics. Each of them played the role of Tarzan during the 1930s. Herman Brix (Bruce Bennett) was a the silver medalist in the 1928 Olympic shot put.

31. Although, Trace Atkins played Defense End for Louisiana Tech University, Toby Keith played Tight End for a USFL team called the Oklahoma City Drillers. Therefore, they could not play against each other.

32. If they had been close in age, Brian Dennehy, Ed Harris and Matthew Fox would have been football teammates at Columbia University. Brain played an alien in Cocoon, Ed played an engineer who met an alien in The Abyss, and Matthew was the star of the TV show Lost.

33. Although they are not close to the same age, science fiction movie star Vincent Price and Incredible Hulk star Edward Norton rowed for Yale. Norton also rowed for Yale during a time when CNN anchor Anderson Cooper would have coxed for the team.

34. Eleanor Holms Jarrett was on her way to the 1936 Games in Berlin to defend her title in the backstroke when she was removed from the team by the Olympic Committee because they did not approve of her assumed partying lifestyle. A couple of weeks later, after training for the 400 meter relay, Marty Glickman and Sam Stolar were replaced by Jesse Owens and Ralph Metcalfe by the Olympic Committee for questionable reasons that appeared to be because of their ethnicity as Jews.

35. Kip Moore played college golf at Valdosta State University around the time Jake Owen played for Florida State University. If they did not compete against each other during college, they probably did in other tournaments.

36. Congressman Steve Largent and Phil McGraw (Dr. Phil) each played football at the University of Tulsa. However, Phil was injured and returned to Texas to finish his education before Largent began playing.

37. Although, Eleanor Holms Jarrett was removed from the 1936 Olympic team on the boat ride to Berlin, she was a member of the team with Olympic decathlon champion Glenn Morris, who played the role of Tarzan with Eleanor Holms Jarrett as the female co-star in the movie.

38. John Layfield, Dwayne Johnson, Tyler Maine, Paul Wight, Kevin Nash and many other professional wrestlers are TV personalities and in the movies.

39. As the son of a senator, vice president Al Gore played basketball and threw the discus for St. Albans High School in Washington D. C. during the 1960s. During the 1970s, actor Clancy Brown, who was the son and grandson of Ohio congressmen, threw the discus for St. Albans before throwing for Northwestern University.

40. Congressman and 1985 Harvard quarterback, Ron Kind worked summers during college for Senator and former Yale athlete William Proxmire, who during the late 1930s was coached by President Gerald Ford.

41. Although, he was a couple of years ahead of Congressman Steve Largent in school, Senator John Boozman, would have played at least one year at the University of Arkansas against Largent, who played college football for the University of Tulsa.

42. Congressman Jim Ryun and Actor Bruce Jenner were track teammates during the 1972 Olympic Games. Maryland congressman Tom McMillen played on the 1972 Olympic basketball team and because of the controversy over a

suspicious few seconds on the time clock, the basketball team has never accepted their silver medal. McMillen was also the NBA teammate of Senator Bill Bradley, a member of the 1964 Olympic basketball team.

43. Congressman Jim Ryun was also in the 1964 Olympic Games with Senator Bill Bradley, who was on our basketball team and Senator Ben Campbell was on our Judo team.

44. Congressman Mike Kelly played football for Notre Dame during the late 1960s, before Reb Brown and Tim Rossovich graduated from USC. Notre Dame and USC often played football against each other.

45. Senator Bill Bradley, Congressman Tom McMillen, Chuck Connors, Shaquille O'Neal, Rick Fox, and Marques Johnson played basketball in the NBA and Marc Blucas played professional basketball in Europe.

46. Congressman J.C. Watts and Eric Alan Kramer played Canadian Football around the same time.

47. Senator Bill Bradley and Congressman Jim Leach were athletes at Princeton during the same time.

Athletes who played in movies together.

1. Mark Harmon played quarterback for UCLA, and co-starred, in Crossfire Trail with former USC basketball player, Tom Selleck. Like Crossfire Trail, Harmon also played a villain in Wyatt Earp, with former CSU-Fullerton baseball player, Kevin Costner, as Wyatt Earp, and former Bellevue College basketball player, Jim Caviezel as Warren Earp.

2. Kevin Costner starred in the movie, Field of Dreams with former circus performer Burt Lancaster. Many years earlier, Burt Lancaster had played the role of Wyatt Earp, with a well-known actor and former wrestler named Kirk Douglas.

3. Kirk Douglas also starred in the War Wagon with former USC football player, John Wayne, and in The Villain with the world's most famous body builder, Arnold Schwarzenegger.

4. Former USC football player, John Wayne has been in many movies. More than once, one of his co-stars was former NFL football star Mike Henry, who was best known for Tarzan movies. However, Wayne played in numerous movies with his former USC football teammate, Ward Bond, who may hold the record for appearing in more John Ford movies that anyone.

5. As a former NFL star, Mike Henry played in lots of action movies, including Tarzan. In Tarzan movies, he often played against other great athletes, such as Olympic decathlon champion Rafer Johnson. He also played well in comedies such as Smokey and the Bandit, with a former FSU running back named Burt Reynolds.

6. Since it was filmed in 1960, perhaps the first movie Rafer Johnson played in was Sergeant Rutledge, starring a former UCLA decathlete and professional football player and professional wrestler named Woody Strode.

7. Former FSU football player, Burt Reynolds played in many other movies with other athletes as he did in Smokey and the Bandit, The Longest Yard, and Hooper. In Smokey and

the Bandit II, he played with NFL Super Bowl MVP Terry Bradshaw and Linebacker Mike Henry. His girl-friend in the movie was the step-daughter of former three-sport college athlete named Jock Mahoney. Mahoney is well known for his roles as Tarzan as well as many westerns. While Mike Henry and Terry Bradshaw each played for the Steelers, Henry left football to become Tarzan while Bradshaw was in college at LTU.

8. Perhaps, Jock Mahoney's first TV series was called the Range Rider, which was one of the first TV series produced by Gene Autry. Before playing this role, he played the villain in The Durango Kid, starring former Dartmouth football player, Charles Starrett.

9. Clayton Moore, who played the Lone Ranger, was a former circus performer who began his career as a stuntman, playing villains in Gene Autry movies.

10. Ben Johnson played John Wayne in Chism and The Undefeated, and Hank Worden played in McClintock, as well as The Searchers, along with Ken Curtis.

11. Super heavy-weight martial arts champion, Dolph Lundgren played the Russian boxer In Rocky IV that killed Carl Weathers character (Apollo Creed) in the ring.

12. Former USC javelin thrower, Michael Landon played Little Joe Cartwright, along with his big brother Hoss, played by former Sul Ross State University football player Dan Blocker. Former University of Cincinnati football player David Canary played their top ranch-hand.

13. Former Iowa University swimmer, football, basketball player Jock Mahoney was the Range Rider, with his side-kick, former rodeo cowboy Dick West.

14. Burt Lancaster played the Crimson Pirate, with his side kick and former partner in the circus, Nick Cravat.

15. Former crew athlete, Gregory Peck was leading man in The Big Country and the villain was played by former professional baseball and basketball player Chuck Connors.

16. Shortly, after USC football player Ward Bond died, former UCLA basketball player Denny Miller began co-starring in Wagon Train. We have listed the many athletes on TV's Gunsmoke, as well as the football and track athletes on Bonanza. However, we often saw other former athletes on these shows, such as former college football player Jack Lord, who played in many roles in westerns such as he did on an episode of Laredo, where he shared the stage with multi-sport athlete William Smith. Although, he played the lead in TV's Have Gun Will Travel, former Stanford boxer Richard Boone often played in movies with other athletes such as Randolph Scott and John Wayne. Eight sport college athlete Dale Robertson played in many of these movies as well as his own TV show, Tales of Wells Fargo.

17. Charles Starrett and Jock Mahoney played together in movies as well as the series, The Durango Kid.

18. Jack Palance was a professional boxer and college football player before co-starring with former Marshall University baseball player Billy Crystal in City Slickers.

19. Ted McGinley played a starring role on Hope and Faith. In one episode, his sister-in-law was dating Dean Cain. On the TV show In the Heat of the Night, O. J. Simpson played the role of a former Mississippi football player who played against Bubba Skinner (a starring role, played by Alan Autry) when he played football for Alabama.

Athletes-turned-actor who played the same role.

1. Former professional baseball players Kurt Russell, and college baseball player Kevin Costner, have each played the role of Wyatt Earp, most recently. However, former a race-car driver, James Garner, who is one of the best all-time golfers in Hollywood, has played this role multiple times, and former circus athlete, Burt Lancaster, played this roll before Russell, Costner or Garner played this role.

2. In an early version of Wyatt Earp, undefeated wrestler Kirk Douglas played the role of Doc Holiday, while in the most recent generation, when college baseball player, Kevin Costner played Wyatt Earp, celebrity golf champion Dennis Quaid played the role of Doc Holiday.

3. Johnny Weissmuller and Buster Crabbe were Olympic gold medal swimmers; Jock Mahoney was a college swimmer, as well as a football and basketball player. Glen Morris was the gold medalist in the 1936 Olympic decathlon, as well as a professional football player, and Herman Brix (Bruce Bennett) was the silver medalist in the 1928 Olympic shot put, after he was a tackle for the University of Washington during the 1926 Rose Bowl. Mike Henry played professional football, James Pierce was a college football player,

Denny Miller played college basketball for UCLA, Frank Merrill was a gymnastics champion, and Gordon Scott was a body builder.

4. On the TV series, Days of Our Lives, former Yankees baseball player, Drake Hogestyn and former Dartmouth College quarterback, Josh Taylor have played the role of Roman Brady. Then Drake Hogestyn's character found out he was really, another character, named John Black, and Josh Taylor kept playing Roman Brady.

5. The Flash Gordon movies were made famous by Olympic swimmer Buster Crabbe. However, forty years later an NFL football player, named Sam J. Jones played the role.

6. Five-sport athlete Bo Svenson starred in two of the three original movies, in the Walking Tall trilogy. Thirty years later, professional wrestler Dwayne "The Rock" Johnson, starred in an adaptation of the role, as did four-sport college athlete, Kevin Sorbo.

7. Before, playing the unforgettable role of Darth Vader, 6'7" body builder David Prowse had played the role of Frankenstein. During the 1980s, a young Northwestern University discus thrower named Clancy Brown played the role.

8. In the movies, Conan was played by Mr. Olympia, Arnold Schwarzenegger. In the TV series 6'6" body builder Ralph Moller played this role.

9. In the movies, Mr. Universe, Steve Reeves is best known for playing Hercules. However, Arnold Schwarzenegger

and Lou Ferigno have each played the role. One of the most popular TV series' of all time starred Kevin Sorbo, as Hercules.

10. While William Smith played the role of Kull the Conqueror in Conan the Barbarian, nearly 20 years later, the prequel to Conan was made starring Kevin Sorbo, as Kull.

11. Hardin-Simmons football player, Fess Parker, played Davey Crocket as well as Daniel Boone, while USC football player, John Wayne played the role of Davey Crocket in The Alamo, and heavyweight boxer George Montgomery played the role as well.

12. The role of Chester was played by All-American decathlete from the 1948 Olympic Trials named Dennis Weaver. Afterwards, rodeo cowboy Ken Curtis, placed the role of Festus, and FSU football player Burt Reynolds played the Dodge City blacksmith.

13. Several football players have played in the two editions of The Longest Yard. In the first movie, professional football player Mike Henry played a guard, while FSU football players Burt Reynolds and Sonny Shroyer played inmates. In the more recent movie, professional football player Brian Bosworth played a guard, while professional football player Terry Crews played an inmate. Other NFL football players in the 1974 version included Ray Nitschke, Jim Nicholson, Pervis Atkins, Joe Kapp and Ernie Wheelwright, and University of Washington quarterback, Sonny Sixkiller. Other NFL football players in the 2010 version included Michael Irvin. In this version, there were several wrestlers and mixed martial arts athletes. Wrestlers included Kevin

Nash, Steve Austin, Bill Goldberg and The Great Khali and Bob Sapp who is also known for Mixed-Martial Arts.

14. Hardin-Simmons football player Fess Parker played Daniel Boone on TV. However, WWI Navy boxing champion George O'Brien and Olympic shot putter Herman Brix (Bruce Bennett) played the role before TV was invented.

Athletes who played athletes and coaches in the movies

1. Former USC basketball player Tom Selleck played the role of President David Eisenhower, who was a great football and baseball player at West Point.

2. Burt Lancaster, a former circus performer played many roles as an athlete. He is well known for his role as the great Olympic and professional athlete, Jim Thorpe. Shortly, before his death, Lancaster played in the movie, Field of Dreams, as former professional baseball player-turned-medical doctor, Archie "Moonlight" Graham.

3. Congressman and Olympic decathlon champion Bob Mathias played himself in a movie about Bob Mathias.

4. California Governor and Mr. Olympia, Arnold Schwarzenegger played the role of the famous bodybuilder, Mickey Hargitay in a movie about Mickey and his wife, Jane Mansfield.

5. Chicago Bears lineman, Alex Karris played in many athletic roles, including former Professional wrestler, Zaharius, in a movie about him, and his famous wife, Babe Dietrick-Zaharius, who was thought to be the greatest female athlete of the first half of the 20th century.

6. Most everyone remembers the movie, Brian's Song, about Brian Piccolo who played full-back for the Bears, with his close friend Gayle Sayers as the half-back. The actor who played the role of Brian Piccolo was James Caan, a former Michigan State University football played, who became a professional rodeo cowboy before playing in this memorable role. Later, he would play a head football coach in The Program.

7. Many former football players have played football coaches in the movies. They know the plays and what they mean. This was evident when former Columbia University wide receiver, Matthew Fox played the role of Coach Red Dawson, in We Are Marshall.

8. Jim Caveizal, a former college basketball player, best known for playing Jesus in the Passion of Christ played the role of professional golfer Bobby Jones.

9. Like Matthew Fox, former Florida State University football player Sonny Shroyer was an excellent choice to play the role of Coach Bear Bryant, in Forest Gump. Being from Georgia, he probably grew up in an atmosphere dominated by stories about the famous Alabama coach.

10. We all know him as Al Bundy, from Married with Children. But his real name is Ed O'Neil, who played college football for Youngstown State University, before going to the Pittsburg Steelers where he did not make the final cut, and returned to Youngstown to teach high school before becoming a movie star. Ed is often seen in movies playing the role of a football coach in Little Giants, or an Olympic track coach in the Steve Prefontaine Story.

11. Olympic decathlon champion Bruce Jenner played in the John Capelletti Story. Few people know that Bruce was also a college football player and a water ski champion.

12. David Keith has played in many action roles. However, one of his first starring roles was when he played a decathlete in the 1980 Olympics, in The Golden Moment.

13. As a champion Judo athlete (among other sports), and former marine, playing the role of former professional wrestler Buford Pusser in Walking Tall Parts 2, and 3 came natural for Bo Svenson.

14. Tommy Lee Jones played the role of Ty Cobb after playing football for Harvard. He is also well known for being so good on horseback that directors had to ask him not to do dangerous stunts in westerns such as Lonesome Dove.

15. Kurt Russell comes by sport in a big way. His father was a professional baseball player turned actor. Then Kurt was a child actor until he left to play professional baseball, only returning after an injury ended his baseball career. Although, he can no longer play pro ball, he has played in more than one movie about sports, including Miracle, where he played the role of the 1980 US Olympic Hockey coach.

16. Kevin Costner has played in more movies about sport than most actors. As a former college baseball player, he is well known for his many roles as a baseball player.

17. Ward Bond was a football player for USC along with his teammate, John Wayne. During The 1950s, he played the role of Bob Mathias' high school track coach.

18. Before he was the President of the United States, Ronald Reagan was also a movie star who played in roles as a college football player as well as a professional baseball player.

19. Dennis Quaid has played in many roles as athletes, including baseball and football as well as surfing. One of his most memorable characters was a true story about the Tampa Bay Rays pitcher, Jimmy Morris.

20. Many movies have been made about sport. Some of them include Blue Chips, where Jim Caviezel and Shaquille O'Neal played two of the basketball players. In the Longest Yard several professional football players such as Mike Henry and Terry Crews played in the roles. Alan Autry played in North Dallas Forty, Burt Reynolds and Kris Kristofferson played in Semi-Tough. Tim Rossovich, Kevin Costner, Forry Smith, Marc Blucas, Jeff Severson, has played in a long list athletic roles During the 1920s and 30s, Charles Starrett and Herman Brix (Bruce Bennett) have played athletes in their early movies, before they were big stars.

Answers to Who's in the News

1. Eric Bolling played baseball for the Pittsburg Pirates, Adam Housley played for the Brewers, and Bill O'Reilly played semi-pro for the Monarchs.

2. Boston College softball player, Elisabeth Hasselbeck, the wife of Tim Hasselbeck and sister-in-law to Matt Hasselbeck is an anchor on Fox and Friends.

3. Fox and Friends anchor, Brian Kilmeade played soccer for C.W. Post College.

4. Fox News anchor, Bob Beckel played football for Wagner College.

5. Fox News anchor, Bill Hemmer was ready to play football for Division III colleges but thought Miami of Ohio would be less expensive.

6. Academic All-American Swimmer Laurie Dhue was a reporter for Fox News.

7. Jack Hanna left his home in eastern Tennessee to play football at Muskingum College in Ohio before becoming the read Tarzan on Animal Planet.

8. CNN anchor Anderson Cooper coxed for the Yale crew team during the time Ed Norton was on the team.

9. CNN anchor Erin Burnett played lacrosse and field hockey for Williams College.

10. Network News anchor, Robin Roberts played basketball for SELSU in Louisiana, before the university became the University of Louisiana at Hammond.

11. John Tesh played mid-field in soccer for NCSU.

12. Robert Gibbs played goalie in soccer for NCSU.

13. To name a few sportscasters who have been in the movies, we can begin naming NFL athletes Terry Bradshaw, Phil Simms, and Howie Long. Tennis player Cathy Lee Crosby, college football players, Kurt Herbstreet and Burt Reynolds FSU teammate Lee Corso. One name we have to include would also be Marty Glickman, a member of the 1936 Olympic track team.

CHAPTER 6

POP STARS AND POLITICIANS TAKE THE FIELD.

The following quiz questions are designed to test your knowledge concerning the many athletic relationships among TV and movie icons, musicians, and members of the federal government. The last pages of this chapter are made up of cross word puzzles concerning these personalities. The answers to each quiz are listed in chapter seven.

1. What uncommon relationship does President Gerald Ford and Congressman Bob Mathias share with actors Mark Harmon and Johnny Mack Brown?

2. What unique relationship does President Gerald Ford have with Senators Robert Taft Jr. and William Proxmire?

3. What unique relationship does President Gerald Ford have with Congressman Tom Osborne?

4. All three of the U.S. presidents who cut income taxes were multi-sport athletes during college. Who are they and what were their sports?

5. Among the three presidents named in the previous question, which ones played two of the same sports during college?

6. What sports do Presidents Kennedy and Reagan have in common with TV and movie star Ted McGinley and Fox New Anchor Laurie Dhue?

7. Other than being former college athletes, what does TV and movie star Clancy Brown, and TV and pop music star Billy Ray Cyrus have in common with President George Bush?

8. How does President Ronald Reagan's life parallel with Congressman J.D. Hayworth.

9. How does President Ronald Reagan's life parallel with Governor Arnold Schwarzenegger?

10. What did professional baseball player Archibald Graham have in common with Jesse Ventura?

11. After South Carolina native, Senator John Edwards played wide receiver for Clemson University's football team he transferred to North Carolina State University to finish his undergraduate degree. Shortly after he graduated, a young man played football for NCSU, became a sports caster near Senator Edwards' hometown, and became a Congressman for the state of Arizona. Who was this man?

12. Shortly after the Arizona congressman named in the previous statement left NCSU, a former white house press secretary played goalie for their soccer team. Who was he?

13. A native of North Carolina moved to Charlotte after playing football for Georgia Tech University. He later became one of the most memorable actors in western movies. When he died, he was buried in his hometown of Charlotte, NC, where his good friend Billy Graham preached at his funeral. Who was this movie icon?

14. How did Senator John Edwards' sports and political career parallel with Congressman Heath Shuler?

15. Which member of congress played basketball in the state where he shared the state with Congressman Heath Shuler?

16. Which star of the TV show Necessary Roughness, played college basketball in the state of North Carolina before he played professional basketball in Europe?

17. What is the unique relationship that Congressman Heath Shuler and actor Mark Harmon each share with Senator George Allen?

18. What does Senator Paul Wellstone have in common with Fox News Anchor Laurie Dhue?

19. President Abraham Lincoln and Congressman Dennis Hastert are natives of the same state. But what sport did they share? Congressman Hastert was a college athlete and President Lincoln was a professional.

20. Which current congressman from Ohio was a two-time NCAA champion in the sport performed by President Lincoln, Secretary of Defense Donald Rumsfeld, and Congressman Hastert?

21. What sport does CNN journalist Anderson Cooper share with Fox journalist Geraldo Rivera?

22. What unique occurrence in sport did the actor, Kirk Douglas share with Secretary of Defense, Donald Rumsfeld?

23. Kirk Douglas and Woody Strode fought each other, as gladiators in the movie, "Spartacus". What sport did they share?

24. What professional sport did President Teddy Roosevelt share with actors Bob Hope, Reb Brown, Tony Danza, and Jack Palance?

25. One of our recent Senators played baseball for the Old Mill teams in Georgia, Tennessee, and North Carolina, became a college baseball coach at Young Harris College, the Governor of Georgia, then returned to Young Harris College, and became a U.S. Senator for the state of Georgia before retiring. Who was this athletic politician?

26. What professional sports organization does actor Chuck Connors share with Senator Pete Domenici?

27. Actor Chuck Connors arguably, has the best story in Hollywood, concerning how he left professional sports to become a TV and movie star. It has been told on numerous TV shows. What is this interesting story?

28. What unique relationships, in sport, did Congressman Bob Mathias share with actor Bill Cosby?

29. While Iowa University rarely played Kansas University in football and basketball, Senator Bob Dole may have played in one

or both of these sports against a famous actor who played in Tarzan movies, as well as the Range Rider. Who was he?

30. What TV and movie star competed against Congressman Bob Mathias in the 1948 Olympic Trials?

31. What rodeo cowboy replaced the movie star named in the previous question, on one of the most famous TV shows of all time? This cowboy was also a movie star, as well as a musician.

32. What sport does actor/model Brad Johnson have in common with actor Ben Johnson?

33. What actor who is most famous for his role as a comic book character held an NCAA record for interceptions in football that probably included interceptions from Congressman Ron Kind, who played quarterback for Harvard, and kept another actor who recently played the comic book character known as "Racer X" from catching the ball, as a wide receiver from Columbia University.

34. What Congressman from Indiana was playing basketball at a college about 50 miles south of where Senator John Edwards was playing football?

35. What Defensive End for the Rams became a major TV star during the early 1980s, and was born the same day as President George W. Bush?

36. What do Senator Bob Dole and Congressman Jim Ryan have in common with Actor Bruce Dern and British Parliament member Sebastian Coe?

37. Name the athletes in this book who played professional football against Congressman Steve Largent.

38. Name the TV psychologist who played football for the same university as Congressman Largent.

39. Name the two members of Congress who played basketball for the New York Knicks.

40. Since the University of Idaho often played against North Arizona University, during the late 1970s and early 1980s, which congressman and actor (currently known as the voice for the cartoon character, Patrick Star), would have played against each other in college football?

41. Since the University of Idaho and Louisiana Tech University played each other in football, which of the football players named in the previous question would have played football against a defensive end from LTU, who became a major country singer? And who is this tall, athletic, country singer who played for LTU?

42. Since a quarterback from Tennessee would have played against Florida State University, around the time FSU went to the Sugar Bowl, which Congressmen would he have played against and who was this quarterback? Neither of them are congressmen for Tennessee or Florida.

43. Other than playing roles in Tarzan movies, what event did Johnny Weissmuller share with Buster Crabbe and Herman Brix (Bruce Bennett) in 1928?

44. Other than playing the roles in Tarzan movies, what event did Buster Crabbe share with Eleanor Holms Jarrett, in 1932?

45. What does Eleanor Holms Jarrett have in common with Australian Parliament member Dawn Frazer?

46. If the two ladies referred to in the previous question, preferred to be interviewed by a female news anchor that competed in their sport during college, who might be the best choice?

47. What sport does TV sportscaster Cathy Lee Crosby share with pop singer Lionel Ritchie?

48. Which movie star played football for the university where actor Parnell Roberts attended, and later starred in a movie with Roberts, before the TV show Bonanza premiered?

49. Name five celebrities in this book who were pop stars before and after they were national or world class athletes?

50. Name the actor who was a child actor, then left to become a professional baseball player, before an injury ended his baseball career and he returned to acting. He is also the son of a professional baseball player who became an actor, after he was injured. Name both of these father-and-son athletes-turned- actors.

51. What does Senator Jack Kemp have in common with the man who has been the mayor of Fresno, California, for the past several years?

52. What does the mayor of Fresno, California, have in common with the governor of California, and a former governor of California, who became President of the United States?

53. What do actors Dean Cain, Burt Reynolds and Forry Smith have in common that changed their expected careers?

54. What does Senator Bill Bradley have in common with actor Dean Cain?

55. Other than being college athletes, what common bond did Senator Bill Bradley share with Congressman Tom Allen?

56. What does Senator Pete Domenici have in common with actor Kurt Russell?

57. Why do the years 1953 and 1954 imply a unique relationship between the careers of Senator Pete Domenici and actor Chuck Connors?

58. What relationship concerning their teenage choices in sport does actor Miles O'Keefe and Animal Adventure host Jack Hanna share?

59. What acting role did Miles O'Keefe play that gave him another relationship with Hanna?

60. What unique relationship in sport does the actor Kevin Sorbo share with sportscaster and former Super Bowl MVP, Phil Simms that would cause one to think they were college teammates?

61. During the late 1930s, the 1936 Olympic gold medalist in the decathlon played the role of Tarzan. However, 30 years later, the 1960 Olympic gold medalist in the decathlon, played the role of villains in Tarzan movies. Who were these two world champions?

62. If the 1960 Olympic gold medalist in the decathlon was playing villains in the Tarzan movies of the late 1960s, who was playing Tarzan?

63. The decathlete mentioned in the previous question graduated from UCLA. However, another decathlete who graduated from UCLA, over twenty years earlier, began playing villains in Tarzan movies during the 1950s, and continued to do so during the 1960s. Who was he?

64. Name the college and professional football players who played the role of Tarzan, in the movies.

65. During the early 1960s, a body builder was playing Tarzan. The villain in one of his movies was a former competitor of his sport, from another country. This actor placed third in the Mr. Universe contest, and later turned down the role of Tarzan to become a house-hold name as another movie character. If he had played the role of Tarzan, he would have been the only actor to play this role, who was a native of the country where the Tarzan character's family lived. Who is he?

66. After the body builder named in the previous question became an actor, a very large man from his country won the national title for body building, giving him many roles such as Darth Vader, in the movie Star Wars. Who is he?

67. What character in a movie does the body builder who played Darth Vader in Star Wars have in common with a discus thrower from Northwestern University who is most famous for playing the role of Kurgan in the first Highlander movie, and is also the voice for Mr. Krabs, in the popular animated movie, SpongeBob Squarepants?

68. What does the Northwestern University discus thrower named in the previous question, have in common with Vice President Al Gore? They actually share two relationships. However, they are for the same reason. Name the actor and both of the relationships.

69. The Northwestern University discus thrower, named in the previous question, shares a similar relationship with a half-miler from the University of Pennsylvania, as well as another unique relationship. Who are these two former track athletes and what are these relationships?

70. The actor named in the previous question also shares a unique relationship with a football player from the University of Idaho, who became an actor and then the voice of a famous cartoon character. Name these two very large, athletic men, and their unique relationship.

71. What do actors Rafer Johnson and Woody Strode have in common?

72. What do actors Rafer Johnson and Denny Miller have in common?

73. What do actors Woody Strode and Dennis Weaver have in common?

74. What does Congressman Bob Mathias have in common with actor Bo Svensen?

75. What does Senator Ben Campbell have in common with Bo Svenson?

76. What sport do actors Kevin Sorbo and Bo Svenson have in common with Canadian Parliament member Howie Meeker?

77. What career did Burt Lancaster share with Clayton Moore before becoming stuntmen and movie stars?

78. What record did actor Dean Cain hold in college that could have stopped Congressman Steve Largent gaining a record in professional sports?

79. If Dean Cain had not been injured, he would have played for the same professional sports team as which U.S. Senator?

80. Dean Cain played the role of Superman on TV. Which silver medalist in the Olympics was a congressman for the state where the Superman character grew up?

81. A former FSU football player starred in a movie about a stunt coordinator, called, "Hooper". Shortly after the film aired, a former EKU football player starred in a TV series about a stunt coordinator. The TV series was titled, "The Fall Guy". Who were these two athletes?

82. Name the TV and movie stars in this book, who lost their football scholarships, due to an injury and returned to their home state to finish their college education?

83. Name the TV and movie stars in this book, who became movie stars shortly after being injured and leaving their perspective colleges.

84. Name some of the congressmen and pop stars whose sports careers were ended by WWII.

85. Name the two movie stars who lost their track and field scholarship because of the length of their hair.

86. What position in sport do Senator Jack Kemp, Senator George Allen, Congressman Ron Kind, Congressman Heath Shuler, news anchor Bill O'Reilly, and actors Alan Autry, Mark Harmon, George Lindsey, and Josh Taylor, all have in common?

87. What professional sport do Senators Jim Bunning and Pete Domenici share with actors Chuck Connors, Drake Hogestyn, Bing Russell, and Kurt Russell, as well as country music star Charlie Pride, and new reporter Adam Houlsey?

88. What TV character was played by third baseman for the Yankees, and the University of South Florida, as well the quarterback for Dartmouth College? Who are these two actors?

89. What do President John Kennedy, Senator Edward Kennedy, Senator Robert Taft, Jr., Senator William Proxmire, and Congressman Ron Kind have in common with actors Dean Cain, Tommy Lee Jones, Charles Starrett, Josh Taylor, Matthew Fox and Ed Harris?

90. What college sport event does Terry Bradshaw share with Michael Landon, Garth Brooks, and Bill Cosby?

91. Name the U.S. congress men who competed in the same three college sports as Bill Cosby.

92. What college sport event does Rosie Greer share with Clancy Brown?

93. What does Congressman Rob Simmons have in common with Bruce Dern and Bill Cosby?

94. Three other celebrities have a similar relationship to that of the three mentioned in the previous question. Two of them are famous country musicians and one played a deputy sheriff on one of the longest running TV show. Who are they and what relationship do they share?

95. Three actors have a closer relationship, regarding sport than the one made in the previous question. One was a college football player who became a western star before WWII, one was a college football quarterback who plays a well known character on a day-time soap opera, the third athlete was a college and professional soccer player who played on the night-time soap opera "Melrose Place". Name this unique relationship shared by these three TV and movie stars.

96. In respect to the previous question, what does Senator Bob Dole have in common with Congressman Jim Ryun?

97. Two professional athletes have an even closer relationship than that of Bob Dole and Jim Ryun. One played NFL

football for the Rams, during the late 1960s, through the 1970s, before becoming a TV icon in the 1980s, the other played for the Raiders, during the early 1970s, and left football earlier, to co-star in four "Rocky" movies. Who are they and how did they have a closer relationship in sport than Bob Dole and Jim Ryun?

98. What does Bill O'Reilly have in common with country music star Roy Acuff and actor Timothy Busfield?

99. With respect to the athletes-turned-entertainers in the previous question, what do actors Forrest Tucker and William Smith have in common?

100. The actor who played Jesus, in "The Passion of Christ" played basketball for Bellevue Community College. His father played for UCLA under the same coach as one of the actors who played the role of Tarzan, in the late 1950s, followed by the TV series "Wagon Train". Who are these very athletic movie stars?

101. What world class athlete, in five sports, taught meta-physics at UCLA while playing the role of former wrestler-turned-Tennessee sheriff Buford Pusser, in the two sequels of the "Walking Tall" trilogy?

102. Why were Congressmen John Tanner and Ander Crenshaw rivals during college?

103. If Bill Cosby had started his college career 25 years later, what professional football player on the TV show "Everybody hates Chris" would have been tackling Cosby in the MAC championships?

104. What does Congressman Jason Altmire have in common with actors Burt Reynolds, Sonny Shroyer and Robert Urick?

105. What do actors Matthew Fox and Billy Crystal have in common?

106. What Stetson University basketball player made his body size into a marketable character on the 1960s sitcom, "The Adams family"?

107. What does the actor in the previous question have in common with Congressman Ander Crenshaw?

108. With respect to the previous question, how might Congressman Crenshaw's career path relate to that of actor Sonny Shroyer?

109. Billy Ray Cyrus was a college athlete. What U.S. senator was a professional athlete in the same sport in which Cyrus competed in college? This senator represented Cyrus' home state of Kentucky.

110. What does talk show host and musicians John Tesh and Jim Sonefeld have in common with actors Andrew Shue and Eric Cantona?

111. What does TV show host Geraldo Rivera have in common with Congressman Dutch Ruppersberger?

112. What movie star in An Officer and a gentleman went to the University of Massachusetts on a gymnastics scholarship?

113. Slim Pickens, Hank Worden and Ken Curtis often played comic relief characters in westerns. What sport do they have in common?

114. Name a stand-up comedian who competed in the same sport as the athletes in the previous question.

115. Ricky Nelson was a famous TV star and pop singer during the 1960s and 70s. Although, he is not famous for playing football, he was surrounded by college and professional football players in his family. Name some of these men.

116. Although, Ricky Nelson did not star in many westerns, in Rio Lobo, he co-starred with at least two for USC college players from the 1920s, as well as an a well known professional football player from the early 1960s who is famous or playing the role of Tarzan, in the movies. Name these three athletes-turned-actors.

117. Golf Digest often lists the top golfers in Hollywood. Name the entertainers, listed in this book, who have a handicap less than 8, breaking the score of 80.

118. During the past several years, one athlete-turned-actor has usually been ranked as the best golfer in Hollywood. He was the Missouri state champion when he was a freshman at the University of Missouri, and has regularly broken "par". In tournaments. He was a famous pop singer in the 1980s, but is best known for his starring roles in soap operas, such as Melrose Place. Who is he?

119. According to the editor of Golf Digest (December, 2005), who were the five Hollywood golfers with the best all-time golfing abilities?

120. If the congressmen in this book were the same age, and ran a mile relay against movie stars, who would run for each team.

CROSSWORD PUZZLES

Professional and college baseball players who left the field for the stump or the stage.

Across

1. A Yale pitcher who became the first in his family to be President of the United States. Include his middle initials, with his first and last name. (2).
2. Professional pitcher for the Phillies who became a Senator for Kentucky (5).
3. Disney child actor who became a professional baseball player, and later returned to be a major movie star (9).
4. College Football and semi-pro baseball player anchoring on Fox News and selling lots of books (12).
5. Marshall University baseball player in the movie City Slickers with a heavy weight boxer (15).
6. Georgetown College baseball player who was a major country singer before managing his daughter's successful career (17).
7. College baseball player best known for playing baseball players in movies (21).
8. The U.S. senator who pitched for a Dodgers farm team called the Dukes (25).

Down

1. Popular country singer who played college ball for Northeast Louisiana State University, and is the son of a professional baseball player (3).
2. Former minor league baseball player who played the Sherriff on Bonanza, and whose son followed a similar path (5).
3. Professional baseball player who became one of the top country singers of the 1970s (7).

4. Fox News reporter who played minor league baseball for the Brewers (13).
5. Traded his professional baseball career to be the top soap opera star on "Days of Our Lives" (19).
6. Yale baseball player who owned a professional team before becoming President of the United States. Do not include his middle initial. (21a).
7. Turned in his baseball bat at Moorehead State to fight angry Greek gods (21b).
8. Gave up college baseball to be a superior governor during a class four hurricane (27).

DR. JAMES E. HOLBROOK

Football

Across

1. U.S. Senator and quarterback for the Buffalo Bills (5).
2. All-American at Oklahoma who chose to play Canadian Football before returning to be a U.S. Congressman (7).
3. A college swimmer and football player, sportscaster, movie star, governor, and president. Can't this guy hold down a job (9)?
4. Another college swimmer and football player needing a job as president (11a).
5. Professional defense end and "Hunter" (11b).
6. Mr. Parker was a college football player who often wore a coon skin cap (11c).
7. Professional football player who jogged next to 007's bike and had to go to the "Nerds" party (14).
8. All-American football player who turned down professional football to go to law school while coaching for the university, becoming a decorated naval officer, model, congressman and president. Can any of these presidents hold down a job (16)?

Down

1. Former quarterback for Washington Redskins, returning to Washington as a congressman (2).
2. FSU football player who became "The Bandit" in movies (7).
3. The congressman who held the reception record for the NFL (9).
4. The Dartmouth football player of the 1920s who became a cowboy star in the 1930s (11).
5. The Columbia University wide receiver who gets "Lost" when he is not making major movies, such as Speed Racer, Vanishing Point, and We are Marshall (13).

6. Nominated for the Heisman, in 1972, a few years in the pros, including two super bowls, and then we're off to play cops on TV. Obviously, a man in a hurry (14).
7. Linebacker for the Rams, known for playing Tarzan, and later chasing Burt Reynolds around a football field, and down the road from Texas to Georgia in a police car (17).
8. West Point Football player, commanding officer in WWII and President of the United States (19).

Professional football players turned actors and college football players turned politicians

Across
1. End for Washington and Jefferson, Marine in the Korean War, Congressman (6).
2. Willy was one of the first two African Americans to play for the Rams before he was a professional wrestler and movie star (8).
3. Mr. President played college ball for Harvard (10).
4. George played for USC and Virginia before he was a senator (12).
5. Ben was the tall ex-professional football player trying to kill Conan the Barbarian (13).
6. Played for the Oakland Raiders and played in Rocky movies (15).
7. San Diego Chargers defensive end that played with Chris Rock on TV and in the movies (18).
8. A semi-pro football player who "Should've been a Cowboy". (19).
9. Rick is the congressman who played football against Dauber (21).

Down
1. Sloth played professional football for the Raiders (1).
2. Congressman who would have made more complete passes if Superman had stayed out of the way (5a).
3. F-troop sergeant who played semi-pro football (5b).
4. Chasing Terry on the field, then, calling the game with him and Chris (8).
5. John played wide receiver for Clemson before becoming a senator and running for president (9).
6. Mayor Bubba Skinner played QB for the Packers (11).

7. Bob was a three sport athlete at Kansas before he was a senator who ran for president (13).
8. Congressman Zackary was a Division III All-American with plenty of room for a last name (14).
9. Chuck was senator playing ball for Wayne State, but not running for president (15).

Passers and Receivers

Across

1. The Animal Planet Tarzan from Tennessee played college football (3a).
2. Senator and most valuable player for the Buffalo Bills (3b).
3. MVP in the Rose Bowl who turned down professional football to be a movie star (5).
4. Racer X was "Lost" after playing wide receiver for Columbia (7).
5. Goober played QB for North Alabama (8).
6. All-Pro QB in "Failure to Launch" (9).
7. Played football in his home state before becoming a senator in the bordering state and running for president (10).
8. The half-back from Temple University makes me laugh (12).
9. He moved from USC to be Virginia's QB, and stayed to be their senator (15).

Down

1. Pro Receiver played Flash Gordon in the movies (2).
2. He called plays before he called people patriots and pinheads (5).
3. Back for the Vikings played a cop on Hill Street Blues (8).
4. He came to Washington the first time to play QB. Then he was back as a congressman (9).
5. Bubba played QB for the Packers and became mayor of Fresno (13).
6. Dan Tana played tight end for FSU (15).
7. Congressman played QB for the oldest university (16).
8. The world's greatest athlete played full back for Stanford before becoming a congressman (18).
9. Canadian football QB returns to Oklahoma to be a congressman (21).

Basketball players

Across
1. "Lurch" (6).
2. Campbell University basketball player who became a congressman in his home state (9).
3. UCLA basketball player becomes Tarzan in 1959 (10).
4. Magnum (12).
5. Celtic turned "Rifleman" (14).
6. Kansas basketball player and senator who ran for president (16a).
7. New York Knicks player who became a New Jersey senator and ran for president (16b).
8. CSULA basketball player survived a "Three Dog Night" (18).

Down
1. B-ball player and a college coach in another sport, as well as a Nebraska congressman (2).
2. Hercules played four college sports and is a great golfer (6).
3. Billy the Kid was a country singer from Tennessee who played basketball in Mississippi (8).
4. Indiana congressman who played college ball in South Carolina (9).
5. A Drury College basketball player says, "The Price is Right" (13a).
6. Tennessee congressman who played ball for UT (13b).
7. Another New York Knicks player was a Maryland Congressman (15).
8. Florida congressman who played ball for Georgia (20).

DR. JAMES E. HOLBROOK

Track Athletes

Across

1. Congressman Tom ran track and played football, while Senator George only played football (4).
2. Olympic decathlete playing villains in Tarzan movies (6).
3. He ran for Kansas, ran for the senate, and then, ran for president, in 1996 (8).
4. Tarzan was a silver medalist in the shot put (9).
5. "Chester" was a decathlete in the 1948 Olympic Trials (10).
6. Tarzan won the 1936 Olympic decathlon (11).
7. A hundred year old senator ran track for Clemson (12).
8. Funny MAC high jump champion (15).

Down

1. World's greatest athlete in 1948 and 1952 (3).
2. A discus thrower who makes a fortune playing villains, and the voice for cartoon characters (6).
3. Distance running congressman from Connecticut ran track in Pennsylvania (8).
4. Olympic track athlete and congressman held the high school record in the mile for 36 years (10).
5. Olympic decathlete on CHiPs (11).
6. Senate leader and marathon runner from Nashville (13).
7. Coached another sport before being elected to congress for Nebraska (14).
8. "Little Joe" threw the javelin (17).

DR. JAMES E. HOLBROOK

Boxers and Martial arts

Across

1. George was a cowboy movie star who boxed for the University of Montana (7).
2. Captain America was a professional boxer after playing USC football (8).
3. The Beastmaster is also a martial arts master (10).
4. Boxed in college but received his worst nose injury from a flying chair on his TV show (12).
5. Ollie was a college boxer when he defeated his teammate who became a senator for Virginia (13).
6. Jack was a professional boxer but got his big break when he accidentally punched out an amateur named Brando (14).
7. A military boxing champion who got to fight for the championship in "Any Which Way You Can" (15).
8. A professional boxer before the Wild, Wild, West (19).

Down

1. A professional boxer who played a taxi driver who was a professional boxer (2).
2. "He Man" was a super-heavy-weight European martial arts champ (5).
3. Middle-Weight boxer Packy East performed for the troops with a golf club in his hands (6).
4. A professional boxer who was first in his family to be president (9).
5. A second place Annapolis boxer would be a Senator in 2006 (12).
6. George was a professional boxer turned to cowboy movies (14).
7. First Annapolis boxer to be a senator running for president (16a).

8. First American eighth degree black belt campaigned for Huckabee (16b).

Wrestling and Judo

Across

1. Captain of the Olympic Judo team and a U.S. Senator (2).
2. Undefeated wrestler of the 19th century became president (5).
3. Five spot athlete and Marine "Walking Tall" (6).
4. Sabertooth of the X-Men, and Ajax in Troy (7).
5. John wrestled to support his way through Columbia before becoming the "heart throb" of the 1930s movies (9a).
6. Mork was a high school wrestler (9b).
7. Mr. Speaker was a wrestler for Wheaton College (13).
8. Jesse was governor of Minnesota (17).

Down

1. The Undertaker (2).
2. Pro wrestler went to college with Drake Hogestyn, and got to wrestle Rocky (6).
3. A high school wrestler, college boxer, navy captain, U.S. senator, and maybe president (9).
4. The Rock (12).
5. UNC wrestler and Minnesota senator (15).
6. Doc Holladay was a college wrestler while Wyatt Earp was a circus performer (17).
7. Woody was a professional wrestler when he became a villain in Tarzan movies (19).
8. Mr. Secretary was a wrestler for Princeton and the Navy (22).

Soccer, Lacrosse and Hockey

Across

1. Hootie's drummer played mid-field for South Carolina (2).
2. Even religious leaders are scary when they play goalie (4).
3. High school hockey player ran for president with a wide receiver from Clemson (7a).
4. Maryland congressman played the oldest sport in America for University of Maryland (7b).
5. Another one of Buford Pusser's five sports was hockey (10).
6. Fox and Friends guy, who is not Steve Doocy, but is the author of the most successful book, competing with this one (12a).
7. Eric was the German soccer player who moved from the Rat Patrol to the soaps (12b).
8. How did Hercules play basketball and hockey at Moorehead State? (18).

Down

1. Mork also played high school soccer (4).
2. If college boxing, riding a whale on 60 minutes, and digging up Jimmy Hoffa won't get him killed, maybe college lacrosse will be dangerous enough for him (8).
3. MacGyver played hockey (11).
4. All-American at Dartmouth was a pro soccer player before and after co-starring on Melrose Place (14).
5. Connie's husband on E-TV played mid-field for NCSU before his concert at Red Rock (15).
6. Pro soccer player left the team to "Wake-up Maggie" with a song (17).
7. High school hockey player liked to "Speed" with Sandra Bullock (19).
8. NHL Hockey player in Canadian Parliament (22).

Swimmers and Rodeo Cowboys

Across
1. Jefferson D'Arcy was a water polo player (2).
2. Buck Rodgers was an Olympic swimming champion (3).
3. Tom was a rodeo cowboy as well as a movie star in the 1920s (6).
4. Mr. President was a swimmer at Harvard (7).
5. Laurie was a swimmer at UNC (9).
6. Slim was a rodeo cowboy before "Blazing Saddles" (10).
7. The coach on "The Program" was a college football players and a rodeo cowboy (11).
8. Festus was a rodeo cowboy (13).

Down
1. Mr. Johnson was a steer wrestler before he was a model and movie villain (2).
2. Mr. Johnson was a rodeo champion, then, an actor, then, a rodeo champion, then, an actor in movies like "The Sacketts" (4a).
3. Ms. Holms was an Olympic gold medalist in the backstroke who got to keep her own name when she played "Jane" (4b).
4. Mr. President was the captain of his swimming team at Eureka College (6a).
5. Ron was a rodeo cowboy before he was a Blue Collar comedian (6b).
6. Reba went to college on a rodeo scholarship (9).
7. Hoot was a rodeo cowboy before he did his riding stunts on the silver screen (11).
8. Tarzan and Jungle Jim was one of the greatest swimmers of all time (15).

Entertainers who break 80 in golf

Across
1. Maverick and Rockford (4).
2. Kull the Conquer and the Hercules. This ties him and Bo with five sports (6a).
3. The older Quaid brother (6b).
4. Packy East after making movies (8).
5. Her voice never vibrated when she played golf (11).
6. Dennis was the best in 2005 (mis-spelled with an "e" at the end) (12).
7. Played high school golf, and starred with another good golfer in "A Time to Kill" (15a).
8. Went from swinging a bat to swimming a golf club when he returned to the movies (15b).

Down
1. The soap star that breaks par (3).
2. "It's in the hole" said the "Ghostbuster" (4).
3. Coach (5).
4. Bing (7).
5. Robin, the boy wonder. (11).
6. Hepburn's friend Howard (14).
7. Shaft and a Jedi Master (16).
8. Vince is the best golfer in country music is married to Amy (18).

Multi-sport athletes

Across
1. "Please don't call me Tarzan" (2).
2. The funniest way to go from pro baseball to the movies (4).
3. Left Temple University track, football and basketball to be a comedian (7).
4. Another college track, football and basketball player, who became a college football coach before becoming a senator (9).
5. Congressman Tom ran college track and played football and was a Rhodes Scholar (13a).
6. University of Iowa swimming helped more than football and basketball when he played Tarzan (13b).
7. The Undertaker was a college basketball player for Augustine College, in Texas (15a).
8. Mr. Brooks threw the javelin for OSU and played football in high school (15b).
9. Woody was a decathlete at UCLA, a professional wrestler, and played pro football for the Rams (19),

Down
1. Four college sports at Moorehead State University and a good golfer (2a).
2. University of Arizona lacrosse and boxing was a good preparation for riding a whale on the news (2b).
3. USC football and professional boxing are good preparations to play Captain America (4).
4. The president played rugby and baseball for Yale (7a).
5. Bill, on the Factor, played college football and semi-pro baseball (7b).
6. College swimmer and football player, sportscaster, actor, governor and president (9).

7. World's Greatest Athlete was decathlete, football player, and a congressman (12).
8. Bob ran track and played football and basketball for Kansas before he was their senator (15).
9. Harvard swimmer, football player and golfer, and president (17).

DR. JAMES E. HOLBROOK

Athletes who played comic book characters in the movies

Across
1. Princeton interception record holder who played the man of steel (2).
2. Captain America was a professional boxer who played football for USC (5).
3. Tarzan was a well known stuntman, Marine, and triple sport athlete for University of Iowa (7).
4. Tarzan and Jungle Jim was the greatest swimmer of the early 20th century (10a).
5. Tarzan and Ator played football for Mississippi State University (10b).
6. Tarzan was a silver medalist in the shot put and a football player in the 1926 Rose Bowl (12).
7. Flash Gordon played in the NFL (15).
8. Colossus played football for Gammon University (16).
9. Woody was a villain in Tarzan movies (19).

Down
1. Tarzan played basketball for UCLA (3).
2. Tarzan angered Hitler when he broke the decathlon record during the 1936 Olympics (6).
3. Sabertooth was a professional wrestler (10).
4. Hercules was a four sport athlete for Moorehead State University, in Minnesota (13).
5. Mr. America played Tarzan during the early 1960s (14).
6. Tarzan, Flash Gordon, and Buck Rogers was the gold medalist for the 400 freestyle during the 1932 Olympics (15a).
7. Tarzan of the late 1960s was a linebacker in professional football (15b).

8. Racer X, in Speed Racer played wide receiver for Columbia University (17).
9. Mr. Jones played a villain in a Batman movie (20).

Musicians who were athletes

Across

1. Movie star, arena football team owner, actor, and major country music star played baseball for Northeast Louisiana State University (2).
2. Six foot six defensive end from Louisiana Tech University is a major country star who recently worked for Donald Trump on his TV show (4).
3. The Okee from Muskogee was a professional baseball player (6).
4. Hannah Montana's daddy played baseball for Georgetown College (9).
5. Roy was a semi-pro baseball player and country music star (10).
6. Chuck made a Three Dog Night after the basketball games at CSU-Los Angeles (11).
7. He has friends in lonely places and the Oklahoma State University track and football teams (12).
8. The six letters that is the commonly misspelled last name of a world class yacht racer that was Hungry Like the Wolf (15).

Down

1. Steve was an undefeated distance runner when the year he turned, "Eighteen" (1).
2. Professional soccer player who wanted to know "If you Think I'm sexy" (5).
3. Undefeated high school sprinter running with The Police (6).
4. E-TV's favorite mid-fielder for the NCSU soccer team (8).
5. A mid-fielder for the University of South Carolina drummed for Blowfish (9).

6. Country music star from the 1980s, who played football for Texas Tech University (10)
7. Tom said "Make a Wisk" for basketball, while your brother works for WOLD (13).
8. Billy The Kid became a country music star after playing college basketball in Mississippi (14).

DR. JAMES E. HOLBROOK

Soap Opera – 10 soap stars and 10 musicians

Across

1. Drake played third base for the Yankees before he was a soap star (3).
2. Trace played defensive end for LTU before he sang about me and how I am (5a).
3. Mr. Brooks was an OSU javelin thrower before he sang about thunder (5b).
4. Billy was an MU baseball player before starring on "Soap", as Robert's step brother (7).
5. Josh was the QB for Dartmouth before he was a soap star (9).
6. Charlie was a professional baseball player before he sang about kissing angels (10).
7. Andrew was a professional soccer player before and after he lived at "Melrose Place" (11).
8. Simon was sang about Rio while ride the vehicle he raced (12).
9. Mark played for the NFL before he appeared on Guiding Light (16).
10. David played football for UC before he starred on All My Children (19).

Down

1. The best golfer in Hollywood has played on a few soaps (1).
2. Mr. Johnson has two last names, and played DB for the Steelers and Falcons before he was Doc Reese (3).
3. Billy played college basketball before he "Let 'em be Little" (5a).
4. Billy played college baseball before he "Breakied" his heart, and had Hannah (5b).
5. Chuck was a college basketball player before he realized "One is the loneliest number" (9).
6. Robert played tight end for FSU before he played Billy's step brother on "Soap" (11).

7. South Carolina mid-fielder and drummer (14).
8. A second generation baseball player sings about Native-Americans (16a).
9. John played linebacker for BU before One Live to Live and Guiding Light (16b).
10. Rod was a professional soccer player before he sang about Maggie (18).

DR. JAMES E. HOLBROOK

Westerns

Across

1. An All-American football player, from Alabama, who turned professional football to be an actor (2).
2. An All-American football player and son of a professional football player, who turned down professional football to be an actor (4).
3. Hoot was a rodeo cowboy who became a cowboy in the westerns (5).
4. Tom played college basketball for the same university where John Wayne played football. Now he is thought to be the new representative for Louis L'Amour westerns (6).
5. Mr. Johnson was a world rodeo champion before he became an actor (7).
6. John was a professional wrestler before he wrestled actors in westerns (8).
7. David played football for UC before he was the top hand on the Ponderosa (10).
8. "Chester" placed sixth in the 1948 Olympic trials in the decathlon (11a).
9. George was a professional boxer before he punched out actors in westerns (11b).
10. A champion wrestler who did his own stunts in westerns (13).
11. The Georgia Tech football player so well known for 1950s westerns he was referred to a western comedy in the 1970s (15a).
12. A triple sport athlete in college and one of the best stuntmen, before he became the Range Rider (15b).
13. "Festus" was a rodeo cowboy (17a).
14. Robert was a professional boxer before the Wild, Wild West (17b).

15. This UCLA basketball player played Tarzan before he worked for the Wagon Train (19).
16. George boxed for the University of Montana before he became a western star (20).

Down

1. Since Brad was a steer wrestler in the rodeo before he was an actor, his last name is often confused with another rodeo cowboy who became an actor (1a).
2. John played football for USC before he was the Duke (1B).
3. Lee played football for EKU before he was Heath Barclay (3).
4. He played two professional sports before he twirled a rifle (6a).
5. He was a semi-pro football player before he led F-Troop (6b).
6. Dan played football for Sul Ross State before his family owned the Ponderosa (8).
7. Like other swimmers who played in westerns, he played Tarzan, as well (9).
8. Perhaps the first western star, he was also a rodeo cowboy (10).
9. As a javelin thrower for USC, it seemed odd to call him Little Joe (11).
10. Mr. President was also a multi-sport athlete and a western star (12).
11. A silver medalist in the shot put, Tarzan, and a western star (14).
12. A football player for an Ivy League school and a western star (16).
13. Thought to be the greatest athlete in the movies and liked to enter a saloon through the third floor (17).
14. Football teammate to John Wayne and the wagon-master on Wagon Train (18).

15. It took a professional boxer to play villains, and punching out a star didn't hurt (20).
16. A professional rodeo cowboy, a popular rodeo clown, and an unforgettable star for the westerns, playing in the 1970s comedy western that referred to the actor named in 15a (22).

Congressmen and entertainers who competed against each other in sport

Across

1. Senator from Kansas playing football and basketball against Tarzan when he played for Iowa (4).
2. Triple sport athlete for Iowa mentioned in 4-across who played Tarzan in the movies (6).
3. The World's Greatest Athlete and California congressman who competed against "Chester" during the 1948 Olympic Trials (8a).
4. Senator and NLF quarterback being chased by a "Hunter" (8b).
5. Congressman who was a wide receiver for the Seahawks (10).
6. Chris's dad was a defensive end for the Chargers who had to rush the QB for the Redskins who became a congressman (11).
7. Harvard's QB made passes when Superman did not intercept them for Princeton (12).
8. North Arizona football captain played football against Sponge-Bob's buddy (13).
9. The QB for the Steelers who played against the Seahawks receiver before he was a congressman (16).

Down

1. Sponge-Bob's buddy played football for Idaho and often played North Arizona (2).
2. The "Hunter" played defensive end for the Rams and often had to tackle the Senator who played QB for the Bills (5).
3. Princeton's interception record holder tried to make the Harvard QB's passes incomplete before he could become a congressman (6).

4. "Chester" placed sixth, in the decathlon, won by the future California congressman named in 8a-across (10).
5. The North Carolina Congressman and QB for the Redskins was rushed by Hamburger Eddy (13).
6. Mark was the UCLA QB and competed against USC QB whose father coached the team where Mark's father played professional football. The USC QB became a Senator (15).
7. The USC QB only played against Mark one year, before moving to Virginia to be their QB and Senator (19).

Congressmen or Entertainers who competed against each other in sport

Across

1. Pennsylvania congressman who played college football against the Tennessee congressman, named in 13a-down (5).

2. Cowboy movie star who played in the 1926 Rose Bowl against the shot putter/Tarzan character named in 12-down (7).

3. Tennessee basketball player who played against the Florida congressman, named in 18-down, who played basketball for Georgia (9).

4. UCLA QB known to play doctors, lawyers, and NCIS characters, who played against the USC football player who became Captain America, named in 14-across (10a).

5. The character who played in three major movies, the second year he was "Lost" kept trying to catch the football, through the hands of the Princeton free safety, named in 13b-down (10b).

6. UCLA and Olympic decathlete and villain in Tarzan movies, ran track against the javelin throwing teen-age werewolf from USC, named in 16-across (12).

7. Captain America, referred to in 10a-across (14).

8. Javelin throwing werewolf, named in 12-across (16).

9. Quigley played basketball for USC, which is in the same city as the famous musician, named in seven-down, who played for CSULA (19).

Down

1. Columbia University football player in "The Rock" played against Joey, from "Hill Street Blues", and named in 20-down, before Joey was nominated for the Heisman (4).

2. Country artist and former defensive end for Louisiana Tech University, had to play against the University of Idaho, where "Dauber" had recently finished (6).

3. Played basketball against Quigley before his Three Dog Night (7).

4. Dauber was injured, while playing football for Idaho before he got a chance to play against the only major country singer as big as he is (10).

5. Tarzan played in the 1926 Rose Bowl (12).

6. Heath played QB for Tennessee before he went pro (13a).

7. Dean tried to keep the football away from Matthew (13b).

8. Ander played basketball for Georgia, in the same conference as UT (18).

9. Heisman trophy candidate played for Cornell and against Columbia (20).

DR. JAMES E. HOLBROOK

Former athletes who played in movies together

1. Tom was a USC basketball player before he played the nephew of the actor named in 2a-down, in "The Shadow Riders" (2a).
2. Mark and Mr. Johnson, named in 12-down were villains in a western starring the guy named in 2a-across (2b).
3. Kevin was a college baseball player before he starred in a movie about baseball with the circus performer, named in 4-down (5).
4. Terry played defensive end for the Chargers before he was Hamburger Eddie in a movie with the actor named in 6-down. This movie was a re-make of a movie that starred the actor named in 6-down (6).
5. Sean's was in the Mr. Universe contest before his character, in a movie, was killed by the former Northwestern University discus thrower, named in 10-down (8).
6. Hank was a former rodeo cowboy who co-starred in many westerns with the actor named in 2b-down (10a).
7. Robert was a tight end for FSU before he was hung, in the movie miniseries "Lonesome Dove" by the former Harvard football player named in 11-down (10b).
8. Mike was a professional football player, famous for his Tarzan movies. However, he played in several other movies, including one with the former FSU football players, named in 16-across and 6-down (12).
9. Sonny played a football player in "The Longest Yard with the actors named in 12-across and 6-down. However, he is most famous as "Enos" (16).

Down
1. Mr. Johnson was a rodeo champion before he played Tom's uncle in "The Shadow Riders" (2a).

2. John played in many movies with his for USC football team-mate, named in 8-down, as well as the rodeo cowboy named in 10a-across (2b).

3. A former circus performer who co-starred with Kevin in "field of Dreams" (4).

4. A former FSU football player who played in both version of "The Longest Yard" (6).

5. Former USC football player played in "The Searchers" with the former rodeo cowboy, named in 13-down (8).

6. Clancy was the Northwestern University discus thrower played in role of Kurgan, in the movie, "Highlander" when he killed the body builder named in 8-across (10).

7. Tommy was the former football player at Harvard who played the captain of the Texas Rangers, in the miniseries, "Lonesome Dove" when he had to hang the actor named in 10b-across (11).

8. The former steer wrestler who was a model before he was in a movie where he was hired by the former UCLA QB, named in 2b-across, to kill the former USC basketball player, named in 2a-across (12).

9. Ken was the former singing rodeo cowboy who co-starred in "The Searchers" with John, Hank and Ward (13).

ATHLETES ON THE STUMP AND THE STAGE

Former athletes who played on TV or in the movies together

Across

1. Former circus performer who played with the former wrestler, named in 11-down, in westerns (2a).
2. Mr. Johnson was a former champion rodeo cowboy who played a U.S Marshall, in "Hang 'em High". The track athlete, named in 13-across was a villain in the movie (2b).
3. This former Yankees baseball player not only plays on a soap opera with the Dartmouth QB named in 7a-down, they have each played the same character (4).
4. Jack was a champion golfer in college, and played on a night-time soap opera with the professional soccer player, named in 18-down (8).
5. Jack was a professional boxer before he received an academy award for playing in two sequels with the former Marshall University baseball player, named in 4-down (10).
6. Ted was a water polo player before he became the neighbor of Al Bundy, who is the former football player, named in 13-down (12).
7. The former Penn track athlete who played the villain in "Hang 'em High" (13).
8. In Rocky IV, this former professional football player was killed by the former European kick boxing champion, named in 3-down (16).

Down

1. This former USC track athlete played the brother to the former Sul Ross State University football player, named in 15-down, on the TV show, "Bonanza" (1).
2. Dolph was the kick boxing champion who killed Carl, in Rocky IV (3).

3. The funny former Marshall University baseball player starring with Jack, In "City Slickers" (4).
4. James was a college football player and a rodeo cowboy before he played the role of the coach in "The Program" (6).
5. Josh played more than one role on "Days of Our Lives", including the role formerly played by the former baseball player, named in 4-across (7a).
6. The QB in "The Program" (7b).
7. Doc Holliday played with Wyatt Earp, played by the actor named in 2a-across (11).
8. Al Bundy (13).
9. Dan the Sul Ross state football player who played "Hoss" (15).
10. The pro soccer player on "Mel Rose Place" (18).

CHAPTER 7

ANSWERS TO QUIZZES AND PUZZLES IN CHAPTER SIX

1. They were athletes who turned down professional football contracts to pursue other careers.

2. After turning down opportunities to play for two professional football teams, Ford attended Yale Law School, and coached the football team. Two of the football players he coached were Senator Taft and Senator Proxmire.

3. After playing college sports, they were each college coaches before becoming members of the federal government.

4. President Kennedy was a swimmer, football player and a golfer at Harvard University. President Reagan was a swimmer and a football player at Eureka College. President George W. Bush was a baseball and rugby player at Yale.

5. Kennedy and Reagan were both swimmers and football players. Kennedy also played golf for Harvard, and Reagan was also a cheerleader at Eureka College.

6. They all competed in college water sports. President Kennedy was a swimmer at Harvard, President Reagan was a swimmer at Eureka College, Laurie Dhue was a swimmer at UNC, and Ted Mc Ginley was a water polo player at USC.

7. Their parents were state and federal politicians. President George W. Bush is the son of President George H. W. Bush Clancy Brown is the son of U.S. Congressman Clarence Brown Jr., and Billy Ray Cyrus is the son of Kentucky state legislator Ron Cyrus.

8. President Reagan and Congressman J.D. Hayworth both college football players who became sportscasters before they were members of federal government.

9. President Reagan and Governor Schwarzenegger each were athletes who became movie stars and governor of California.

10. Archibald Graham was a professional baseball player, who returned to his home in Minnesota to return to college and become a doctor. Jesse Ventura was a professional wrestler and actor who returned to Minnesota to be the governor.

11. Congressman J.D. Hayworth played football for North Carolina State University (NCSU) before moving to Arizona to be a congressman. John Edwards played football at Clemson (SC) before transferring to NCSU, and becoming a North Carolina Senator.

12. Robert Gibbs played soccer for NCSU.

13. Randolph Scott was a native of North Carolina, like Billy Graham. He played football for Georgia Tech University. After an injury ended his football career, he finished his education in engineering, and worked in Charlotte. Being slightly older than Graham, he lived near Charlotte when Billy was a teenager. Billy Graham's family owned a dairy

farm and Billy delivered milk to Randolph Scott's home. They later became good friends and golf partners (Graham, 2007).

14. They are each North Carolina congressman who played college football in bordering states. Shuler played for Tennessee and Edwards played for Clemson, in South Carolina.

15. Bob Ethridge played basketball for Campbell University in North Carolina.

16. Marc Blucas played college basketball for Wake Forest University before playing professional basketball in England.

17. Other than the fact, they were all college quarterbacks Senator Allen was a quarterback for UCLA when his father was a coach for the Rams, where Mark Harmon's father played professional football before becoming the head coach. However, Senator Allen transferred to the University of Virginia when his father coached for the Washington Redskins, where Congressman Shuler played professional football.

18. Paul Wellstone was a wrestler and Laurie Dhue was a swimmer at UNC.

19. They were wrestlers. Lincoln was a champion in local matches, and Hastert wrestled for Wheaton College.

20. Congressman Jim Jordan wrestled for the University of Wisconsin.

21. They were crew athletes in college. While Geraldo Rivera rowed for Maritime College during the early 1960s, Anderson Cooper coxed for the Yale team during the late 1980s.

22. They each had undefeated seasons in college wrestling.

23. They were wrestlers. Douglas was a college wrestler and Strode was a professional.

24. They were each professional boxers. Jack Palance made a funny reference to the unique way he became a famous actor involving the way he accidently injured Marlon Brando, while doing a boxing work-out and had to replace him in a movie.

25. Senator Zell Miller, who is quite well known for bringing his ball glove with him to a MLB play-off game and catching a foul-tip, during the game, is one of our most memorable senators.

26. They each played baseball for the Dodgers.

27. During a game, he hit a home run. However, instead of running the bases, he did a fancy walk, or dance to first base, he slid into second base, and did cartwheels to third base. During this time, the third base coach was yelling at him, asking what he was doing. However, Chuck made a funny remark to him and ran to home plate, jumped on the back fence, and acted like a monkey. An entertainment agent was watching the game and called him afterwards, convincing him to leave baseball and become a TV and movie star.

28. They were each college track and field athletes, as well as football players. Winning two Olympic gold medals in the decathlon, Mathias is thought to be the "world's greatest athlete". After being a star in the Rose Bowl, he turned down professional football. Cosby was also a college football player, and like Mathias is best known for track and field. Although, Bill competed in most of the events in the decathlon, he was not known to be a decathlete, like Mathias.

29. Jock Mahoney played basketball, and football, and was also a swimmer at the University of Iowa, before joining the Marines during WWII. After the war, he became one of the best stuntmen in Hollywood, which led him to be an action hero in movie and TV shows, such as Range Rider. In his early 40s, he became the oldest actor to play Tarzan, for the first time. While he was competing at Iowa, a younger, Bob Dole began playing basketball and football at the University of Kansas. However, the sport Dole is most remembered for is track. He came close to setting university records in the 440 and 880, before he had to drop out of college to serve in WWII.

30. Oklahoma decathlete Dennis Weaver took sixth place in the 1948 Olympic Trials. During the 1950s, Weaver became quite famous for westerns. He is best known for his role as "Chester" on the TV western, "Gunsmoke". Twenty years later, he became famous for another character named McCloud". Congressman Mathias was only 17 years old when he won this Olympic Games.

31. After Dennis Weaver left the role of "Chester", in Gunsmoke, a rodeo cowboy and singer named Ken Curtis replaced Weaver, with a similar character, named "Festus".

32. They were professional rodeo cowboys.

33. Princeton University defensive back Dean Cain set the interception records for Princeton, and was supposed to play professional football for the Buffalo Bills, before a knee injury ended his career. He started college before Congressman Kind graduated from Harvard, and was a year ahead of Speed Racer star, Matthew Fox who played wide receiver for Columbia University, another university in the Ivy League conference.

34. While Senator John Edwards only played a wide receiver for a year or two before transferring to NCSU, he is about the same age as Congressman Baron Hill, who played basketball for Furman University, in Greenville, South Carolina, which is about 50 miles south of Clemson.

35. Fred Dryer played college football for San Diego State, before becoming a defensive end for the Los Angeles Rams, until he became a TV star. He is best known for his starring role in the 1980s show called "Hunter".

36. They all ran middle distance. While Congressman Ryun and British Parliament member Sebastian Coe are well known Olympic middle distance runners, Senator Bob Dole and movie star Bruce Dern were very good half-milers during college. Dern ran for the famous track coach and Olympic decathlete Ken Doherty, at the University of Pennsylvania, during the 1950s, and Senator Dole ran for Kansas, during the early 1940s.

37. Congressman Largent played wide receiver from the late 1970s to the late 1980s, setting NFL reception records before

he retired from his thirteen year professional football career. Other professional football players, named in this book, would include: Fred Dryer, Phil Simms, John Matuszak, Terry Bradshaw, J.C. Watts, and Howey Long. Ed Marinaro and Carl Weathers left professional football and began acting around the same time Largent was playing in the NFL.

38. Dr. Phil and Congressman Largent each played football for the University of Tulsa, in Oklahoma.

39. Senator Bill Bradley of New Jersey and Congressman Tom McMillan of Maryland.

40. Congressman Rick Renzi was the captain of the Northern Arizona University football team around the same time TV star Bill Fagerbakke was playing for the University of Idaho. When we see Bill, we think of his role as "Dauber", on the syndicated TV show, "Coach". However, millions of children are more familiar with his voice, as "Patrick Star", the pink starfish on the popular cartoon "Sponge-Bob Square Pants".

41. Country Singer Trace Atkins played football for Louisiana Tech University during the early 1980s. At a muscular 6'6", he played defensive end for LTU. Although, he is only a couple of years younger than Bill Fagerbakke, and they played in the Western Athletic Conference, Bill was injured before his senior year, when he would have played against Trace Atkins.

42. Pennsylvania Congressman Jason Altmire played for Florida State University during in 1989, when they went to the Sugar Bowl. During this time, FSU often played Tennessee,

whose quarterback was Congressman Heath Shuler, of North Carolina.

43. They were Olympic medalists. Weissmuller and Crabbe won many medals in swimming, and Brix was second in the shot put. They played the role of Tarzan during the same time period.

44. Buster Crabbe won the 400 meter freestyle, and Eleanor won the 100 meter backstroke. When Eleanor returned to defend her title in the 1936 Olympics she was banned from the team for controversial reasons, involving curfews, and statements that she trained on champagne and caviar. During an interview, about fifty years later, she said she still liked champagne.

45. They were each Olympic swimmers. Eleanor won the gold medal in the 100 meter backstroke in 1932. Dawn won the 100 meter freestyle, in 1956, 1960 and 1964, becoming the first swimmer, of either gender, to win three consecutive gold medals in the same event.

46. Fox News anchor Laurie Dhue was a swimmer for the University of North Carolina.

47. Cathy Lee Crosby was a professional tennis player. Lionel Ritchie played tennis for Tuskegee University.

48. Randolph Scott played football for Georgia Tech. Many years later, Parnell Roberts, a native of Georgia, attended Georgia Tech. In one of Roberts' first movies, he co-starred in a western called "Ride Lonesome", starring Randolph Scott.

49. Simon LeBond was a world class yacht racer who tried out for the 1988 Olympics after his band; "Duran Duran" had sold millions of records. Actress Geena Davis was in the 2000 Olympic Trials in archery, after she became a major movie star. Kurt Russell was a child actor in Disney movies before he became a professional baseball player. After an injury ended his baseball career, he returned to the movies, where he has been a major movie icon. Andrew Shue was an All-American soccer player at Dartmouth. He started his career as a professional soccer player in Africa. However, he moved back to America and became a TV star in the night time soap opera, "Melrose Place". After he left the show, he played professional soccer for the Los Angeles Galaxy, before returned to the silver screen. Ben Johnson was a champion rodeo cowboy, then, a movie star, then a world champion rodeo cowboy, and returned to the movies, again.

50. Kurt Russell was a child actor, who became a professional baseball player. When he was injured, he returned to the movies.

51. They were professional football quarterbacks before becoming politicians. Senator Kemp was the quarterback for the Buffalo Bills before becoming a U.S. Senator. Fresno Mayor Allan Autry played quarterback for the Green Bay Packers before becoming a TV and movie star. He is best remembered for his role as Bubba Skinner, on the TV show, "In the Heat of the Night". After leaving TV, he returned to his home in California, and became the mayor of Fresno, California.

52. They were athletes and movie stars before they were politicians. Allan Autry played in the NFL before becoming a movie star, followed by his election to the mayor's office in Fresno. Arnold Schwarzenegger was Mr. Olympia, multiple times, before becoming a movie star in Conan the Barbarian. After making many major movies, he was a two-term governor of California. Ronald Ragan was a swimmer and a football player at Eureka College before becoming a TV and movie star. After making many movies, such as "Law and Order", he became the governor of California, followed by two terms as the president of the United States.

53. They each had prospective careers in professional football, playing for the Buffalo Bills. However, Cain and Reynolds were injured before they got a chance to play for their team and Smith was injured after playing a few years. However, that acting thing seems to have worked out for them.

54. They were college athletes at Princeton University.

55. They were Rhodes Scholars.

56. They were minor league baseball players.

57. About a year after Chuck Connors left the Dodgers to become a movie star, Senator Domenici became a pitcher for one of the Dodgers minor league teams.

58. They were football players from Tennessee. Miles O'Keefe left Tennessee to play college ball for Mississippi State University, while Jack Hanna left Tennessee to play football for Muskingum College, in Ohio.

59. Miles O'Keeffe played the role of Tarzan, in the movies. A role in which Jack Hanna lives, as the host for TV's Animal Adventures.

60. They played college football for universities with similar names. Phil Simms played for Morehead State University, in Kentucky, while Kevin Sorbo played for Moorehead State University, in Minnesota (currently, Minnesota State at Moorehead). While Phil graduated around the time Kevin was beginning college, they played about the same time.

61. Glenn Morris won the gold medal in the 1936 Olympics before playing the role of Tarzan. The role of Jane was played by Eleanor Holms-Jarrett, the gold medalist in the 100 meter backstroke, during the 1932 Olympics. However, Eleanor used her own name, in place of "Jane" during the movie. Thirty years later, Rafer Johnson, the 1960 gold medalist in the decathlon played villains in Tarzan movies when Ron Ely and professional football player Mike Henry played the role of Tarzan during that time. Rafer Johnson's children also became world class athletes. His daughter was one of the top professional beach volleyball players.

62. Former Steelers, and LA Rams linebacker, Mike Henry.

63. Woody Strode was not only a UCLA decathlete, he was also a professional wrestler, and played professional football for the Rams.

64. James Pierce played football for Indiana before playing the role of Tarzan during the 1920s. Herman Brix played in multiple Tarzan movies during the 1930s and was not only

a former tackle for the University of Washington, playing in the 1926 Rose Bowl, he was also the silver medalist in the shot put, in the 1928 Olympics. Glenn Morris was not only the 1936 Olympic decathlon champion he also played one season of professional football after playing Tarzan in the movies. During the early 1960s, a football, basketball and swimming athlete for the University of Iowa, named Jock Mahoney played in multiple Tarzan movies. As an Iowa University, athlete of the late 1930s, Mahoney was the oldest actor to play Tarzan, for the first time. Mike Henry played professional football for the Steelers and the Rams, before replacing Mahoney during the mid 1960s, and during the early 1980s, one of the Tarzan movies starred Miles O'Keefe, who played college football for Mississippi State University during the mid 1970s.

65. Sean Connery was a body builder from Scotland, the country where the family of John Clayton, alias "Tarzan", originated. Several years after placing third in the Mr. Universe competition, he played the role of a villain in a Tarzan movie, where the role of Tarzan was played by a body builder named Gordon Scott. Sean turned down the role of Tarzan when he became "James Bond". Although, 40 years have passed, and Mr. Connery has made numerous other movies, he is still best known as 007.

66. At roughly, 6'7 and nearly 300 pounds, David Prowse is a hard man to miss, walking on the street. As Mr. British Isles, he would be a unique character in roles such as Frankenstein, and other Science Fiction movies. He is also one of the top fitness professionals, training movie stars such as Christopher Reeves, when he played Superman.

However, he is best known as the man behind the mask, and did not need any special effects assistance to play the role of Darth Vader, in Star Wars.

67. David Prowse (Darth Vader) and former Northwestern University discus thrower Clancy Brown have each played the role of Frankenstein, in the movies.

68. Since they are both sons of congressmen, Vice President Al Gore and actor Clancy Brown each attended St. Albans Prep School, in Washington D.C.

69. Although, Clancy Brown is the son of a congressman, he is also the grandson of a congressman, as well. Another famous actor, named Bruce Dern, is the grandson of the former governor of Utah, who became the Secretary of War. Each of these former track athletes has also played an assortment of famous villains in movies.

70. Former Northwestern University discus thrower Clancy Brown and former University of Idaho football player Bill Fagerbakke are each voices for cartoon characters. They worked together on the popular movie, "Sponge-Bob SquarePants". Brown is the voice for Mr. Krabs, and Fagerbakke is the voice for Patrick Star.

71. They were both UCLA decathletes who played villains in Tarzan movies. Although, Strode is much older than Johnson, he played in many Tarzan movies around the same time as Johnson. Johnson was the 1960 Olympic decathlon champion. Strode was also a professional football player and a professional wrestler, during the 1940s and 50s.

72. Rafer Johnson was a decathlete at UCLA, while Denny Miller was a UCLA basketball player, during the 1950s.

73. They were college decathletes before they were actors. Strode went to UCLA and Weaver went to Oklahoma. Both of them have played in westerns and other action films.

74. They were both world class track and field athletes who were Marines.

75. They were both world class athletes in the sport of judo.

76. They were hockey players. Sorbo was a college hockey player, Svenson played on a national team, and Meeker played in the NHL.

77. They were circus performers, on the trapeze. This is why they were such good stuntmen.

78. An NCAA record for interceptions. If he had not been injured, he would have played free safety for the Buffalo Bills during the last year Steve Largent played for the NLF, as the wide receiver who held the NFL record for receptions.

79. Senator Jack Kemp had retired from the Buffalo Bills and became a congressman before Dean Cain was supposed to begin playing for the team.

80. The comic book character, superman, is from Kansas. Kansas Congressman Jim Ryun was an Olympic athlete in the 1500 meter run who also ran track for the University of Kansas and held the high school record of the mile, for 36 years.

81. Former FSU football player, Burt Reynolds played the role of stuntman in "Hooper". Soon after that, former EKU football player, Lee Majors had a TV series based on the same type of character, called the "Fall Guy".

82. While many of the actors in this book lost their athletic scholarship due to an injury, many of them either remained at their original university and paid out-of-state-tuition or dropped out of college. However, out-of-state tuition is high, and some of our most famous movie stars had other careers before they became movie icons. Randolph Scott left Georgia Tech's football team to return to his home state of North Carolina, where he finished his degree in textile engineering and had a career before he moved to Hollywood. Sonny Shroyer left the football team at Florida State University and finished his degree in his home state, at the University of Georgia. While attending UGA, he was discovered for modeling jobs. When Dr. Phil was injured, he left the football team at the University of Tulsa, and returned home to Texas, and obviously completed a lot of education, and that education allowed him to become a TV psychologist, with his own show.

83. John Wayne stopped playing football for USC after a shoulder injury. Soon after his injury, he got a job working with actor Tom Mix, helping his physical training. He became a stuntman, then a movie star. Although, Bill Fagerbakke graduated from college after he was injured, he began acting soon after graduation. Dean Cain had graduated from college with a career playing for the Buffalo Bills until a knee injury changed his path, and he began acting. About 30 years earlier Burt Reynolds suffered a similar injury that kept him from playing for the Bills. Forry Smith played a few

years for the Bills before an injury ended his career. Shortly after Gammon University football player Daniel Cudmore was injured, he had a re-occurring role as Colossus, in "The X-MEN".

84. Many athletic careers ended when WWII began. Jack Palance was a successful heavy-weight, professional boxer until he joined the military. Senator Bob Dole was a talented three sport college athlete who was injured during WWII. Jock Mahoney was a talented three sport college athlete who had recently graduated when he joined the Marines to serve in WWII. After the war he became one of the best stuntmen in Hollywood, before becoming a movie star. The exception would be Chuck Connors, who attended college as a multi-sport athlete. He served in the Army during WWII, and became a professional basketball and baseball player, after the war. Many other athletes' career was halted during the war, but not ended.

85. Bruce Dern was kicked off of the University of Pennsylvania track team by Coach Doherty for not cutting his hair. Michael Landon had a unique form of sport psychology concerning his "Samson-like" view of strength when throwing the javelin for USC. The longer his hair, the further he threw the javelin. When his hair was cut, he stopped throwing for USC and became a movie star.

86. They were football quarterbacks.

87. Baseball.

88. New York Yankee and USF third baseman Drake Hogestyn and Dartmouth quarterback Josh Taylor play on a soap

opera called "Days of Our Lives". At one time, each of them has played the character, Roman Brady, and each of them played another character on that show.

89.   They all played football for Ivy League colleges and universities. Both of the Kennedys played for Harvard, as well as Congressman Kind, and Tommy Lee Jones. Senators Taft and Proxmire played for Yale, Charles Starrett and Josh Taylor played for Dartmouth, Ed Harris and Matthew Fox played for Columbia, and Dean Cain played for Princeton.

90.   They were javelin throwers. Garth Brooks threw for Oklahoma State University, Michael Landon threw for USC, Bill Cosby threw for Temple University, and Terry Bradshaw was the national champion at Louisiana Tech.

91.   Senator Bob Dole, Congressman Tom Osborne ran tack and played football and basketball. Congressman Tom Allen ran track and played football, which were to two sports in which Cosby was inducted in the Temple University Athletic Hall of Fame.

92.   They were college discus throwers.

93.   They were track athletes at colleges and universities in the state of Pennsylvania. Congressman Simmons was a distance runner for Haverford College, Bruce Dern was a half-miler at the University of Pennsylvania, and Bill Cosby did several events for Temple University, but was best known for the high jump.

94.   They were athletes at Oklahoma universities. Country musician Garth Brooks threw the javelin for Oklahoma

State University, country musician Reba McIntyre was a barrel racer in the rodeo for Northeastern Oklahoma State University, and Dennis Weaver, Chester, from TV's Gunsmoke, was a decathlete at the University of Oklahoma.

95. They were all athletes at Dartmouth. Charles Starrett was a football player who became a movie star, in westerns, during the 1930s. Josh Taylor played quarterback for Dartmouth before going to law school. Shortly, after becoming a lawyer, he began acting on the TV soap opera, "Days of our Loves". Andrew Shue was an All-American soccer player before becoming one of the stars on the night time soap opera, "Melrose Place". He then returned to professional soccer.

96. They both ran track for the University of Kansas.

97. Fred Dryer, star of TV's "Hunter", and Carl Weathers, Apollo Creed, from the "Rocky" movies was football teammates at San Diego State University.

98. They were semi-pro baseball players.

99. They were semi-pro football players.

100. Jim Caviesel played basketball for Bellevue Community College before becoming a movie star in the role of Jesus, in the movie "The Passion of Christ". Denny Miller played basketball for UCLA during the mid 1950s, before he played Tarzan in the late 1950s.

101. Bo Svenson was an athlete in track and field, judo, hockey, auto racing and yacht racing. He also teaches college

meta-physics. Although, he has played many roles, he is best known for his role as Buford Pusser, in the second and third installments of the "Walking Tall" trilogy.

102. John Tanner played basketball for the University of Tennessee around the same time that Ander Crenshaw played for Georgia. These universities are in the same conference and play each other often.

103. Before actor Terry Crews played football for the NFL team, the San Diego Chargers, he played college football for Western Michigan University. WMU is in the MAC conference with Temple University. Bill Cosby played football for Temple.

104. They played football for Florida State University.

105. Matthew fox was a college football player who played the role of a football coach where Billy Crystal played baseball.

106. Ted Cassidy played basketball for Stetson University before he became a TV icon as Lurch, on the popular TVs how "The Adams Family".

107. Ted Cassidy was a native of West Virginia who went to Stetson University, in Florida, to play basketball. Ander Crenshaw went to the University of Georgia, to play basketball, before returning to his home state of Florida to become a congressman.

108. Congressman Crenshaw played basketball in Shroyer's home state of Georgia, and Shroyer played football, in Congressman Crenshaw's home state of Florida.

109. Senator Jim Bunning of Kentucky played major league baseball for the Philadelphia Phillies. Pop star Billy Ray Cyrus, a native of Kentucky, played college baseball for Georgetown College, in Kentucky, and the son of a state legislator.

110. They were college soccer players. Tesh played mid-field for North Carolina State University, Jim Sonefeld played mid field for the University of South Carolina, Eric Cantona played professional soccer, and Andrew Shue was an All-American at Dartmouth before turning pro.

111. They were college lacrosse players. Geraldo played for Arizona and Rappersberger played for Maryland, the state he represents as a congressman.

112. Richard Gere.

113. They were professional rodeo cowboys.

114. Ron White was a bronc rider from Texas.

115. His father, Ozzie Nelson played college football for Rutgers University, his father-in-law, Tom Harmon was the 1940 Heisman trophy winner and played professional football for the Los Angeles Rams. His brother-in-law, Mark Harmon, was the quarterback for UCLA who turned down professional football to become a movie star.

116. John Wayne was the star of Rio Lobo, and played college football for USC, along with his former college teammate, Ward Bond, who was also in the movie. The villain in the movies was former LA Rams linebacker, Mike Henry.

117. Jack Wagner, Samuel L. Jackson, Vince Gill, Chris O'Donnell, Kevin Sorbo, Randy Quaid, Dennis Quaid, Kurt Russell, Matthew McConaughey, Bill Murray, Hugh grant, and Craig, T. Nelson.

118. Jack Wagner regularly shoots under par. At the end of a TV soap opera series, the show actually used his relationship with golf as a component of the series' ending.

119. Bing Crosby, Bob Hope, James Garner, Katherine Hepburn, and Howard Hughes.

120. Congress: Senator Bob Dole was a great quarter-miler in college, Congressman Jim Ryun was an Olympic middle distance runner, Congressman Bob Mathias was the two-time Olympic Decathlon champion, and the anchor would be Congressman Tom Allen was a great quarter-miler in college. Hollywood: Rafer Johnson, Woody Strode, and Dennis Weaver were decathletes, and the anchor would be Bruce Dern was a great half-miler at the University of Pennsylvania.

ANSWER SHEET TO CROSSWORD PUZZLES

ATHLETES ON THE STUMP AND THE STAGE

Pros and College athletes

Baseball

Across		Down	
2.	GEORGEHWBUSH	3.	TIMMCGRAW
5.	JIMBUNNING	5.	BINGRUSSELL
9.	KURTRUSSELL	7.	CHARLIEPRIDE
12.	BILLOREILLY	13.	ALANHOUSLEY
15.	BILLYCRYSTAL	19.	DRAKEHOGESTYN
17.	BILLYRAYCYRUS	21A.	GEORGEBUSH
21.	KEVINCOSTNER	21B.	KEVINSORBO
25.	PETEDOMENICI	27.	HALEYBARBOUR

Across: President George H. W. Bush, Senator Jim Bunning, Kurt Russell, Bill O'Reilly, Billy Crystal, Billy Ray Cyrus, Kevin Costner, and Senator Pete Domenici
Down: Tim McGraw, Bing Russell, Charlie Pride, Alan Housley, Drake Hogestyn, President George W. Bush, Kevin Sorbo, Governor Haley Barbour

DR. JAMES E. HOLBROOK

Football

Across		Down	
5.	KEMP	2.	SHULER
7.	WATTS	7.	REYNOLDS
9.	REAGAN	9.	LARGENT
11A.	KENNEDY	11.	STARRETT
11B	DRYER	13.	FOX
11C	FESS	14.	MARINARO
14.	CASEY	17.	HENRY
16.	FORD	19.	EISENHOWER

Across: Senator Jack Kemp, Congressman J. C. Watts, President Ronald Reagan, President John F. Kennedy, Fred Dryer, Fess Parker, Bernie Casey, and President Gerald Ford
Down: Congressman Heath Shuler, Burt Reynolds, Congressman Steve Largent, Charles Starrett, Matthew Fox, Ed Marinaro, Mike Henry, President Dwight Eisenhower

ATHLETES ON THE STUMP AND THE STAGE

Football

Across		Down	
6	MURTHA	1	MATUSZAK
8	STRODE	5A	KIND
10	KENNEDY	5B	TUCKER
12	ALLEN	8	LONG
13	DAVIDSON	9	EDWARDS
15	WEATHERS	11	AUTRY
18	CREWS	13	DOLE
19	KEITH	14	SPACE
21	RENZI	15	HAGEL

Across: Congressman John Murtha, Woody Strode, Senator Ted Kennedy, Congressman Tom Allen, Ben Davidson, Carl Weathers, Terry Crews, Toby Keith, Congressman Rick Renzi
Down: John Matuszak, Congressman Ron Kind, Forrest Tucker, Howey Long, Senator John Edwards, Alan Autry, Senator Bob Dole, Congressman Zackary Space, Senator Chuck Hagel

Football

Passers and Receivers

Across		Down	
3A	JACKHANNA	2.	SAMJJONES
3B	KEMP	5.	OREILLY
5	JOHNNYMACKBROWN	8.	MARINARO
7	FOX	9.	SHULER
8	LINDSEY	13.	AUTRY
9	BRADSHAW	15.	URICK
10	EDWARDS	16.	KIND
12	COSBY	18.	MATHIAS
15	ALLEN	21.	WATTS

Across: Jack Hanna, Senator Jack Kemp, Johnny Mack Brown, Matthew Fox, George Lindsey, Terry Bradshaw, Senator John Edwards, Bill Cosby, Senator George Allen
Down: Sam J. Jones, Bill O'Reilly, Ed Marinaro, Congressman Heath Shuler, Alan Autry, Robert Urick, Congress Bob Mathias, Congressman J. C. Watts

Washington or Hollywood Hoops

Across		Down	
6	CASSIDY	2	OSBORNE
9	ETHRIDGE	6	SORBO
10	MILLER	8	DEAN
12	SELLECK	9	HILL
14	CONNORS	13	BARKER
16A	DOLE	13	TANNER
16B	BRADLEY	15	MCMILLAN
18	NEGRON	20	CRENSHAW

Across: Ted Cassidy, Congressman Bob Ethridge, Denny Miller, Tom Selleck, Chuck Connors, Senator Bob Dole, Senator Bill Bradley, Chuck Negron
Down: Congressman Tom Osborne, Kevin Sorbo, Billy Dean, Congressman Baron Hill, Bob Barker, Congressman John Tanner, Congressman Tom McMillan, Congressman Ander Crenshaw

College and Olympic track athlete running to Washington or Hollywood

Across		Down	
4	ALLEN	3	MATHIAS
6	JOHNSON	6	BROWN
8	DOLE	8	SIMMONS
9	BRIX	10	RYUN
10	WEAVER	11	JENNER
11	MORRIS	13	FRIST
12	THURMOND	14	OSBORNE
15	COSBY	17	LANDON

Across: Congressman Tom Allen, Rafer Johnson, Senator Bob Dole, Herman Brix, Dennis Weaver, Glenn Morris, Senator Strom Thurmond, Bill Cosby

Down: Congressman Bob Mathias, Clancy Brown, Congressman Rob Simmons, Congressman Jim Ryun, Bruce Jenner, Senator Bill Frist, Congressman Tom Osborne, Michael Landon

Boxing and Martial Arts

Across		Down	
7	MONTGOMERY	2	DANZA
8	BROWN	5	LUNDGREN
10	SINGER	6	HOPE
12	RIVERA	9	ROOSEVELT
13	NORTH	12	WEBB
14	PALANCE	14	OBRIEN
15	SMITH	16a	MCCAIN
19	CONRAD	16b	NORRIS

Across: George Montgomery, Reb Brown, Marc Singer, Geraldo Rivera, Oliver North, Jack Palance, William Smith, and Robert Conrad
Down: Tony Danza, Dolph Lundgren, Bob Hope, President Teddy Roosevelt, Senator James Webb, George O'Brien, Senator John McCain, Chuck Norris

Wrestling and Judo

Across		Down	
2	CAMPBELL	2	CALAWAY
5	LINCOLN	6	BOLLEA
6	SVENSON	9	MCCAIN
7	MANE	12	JOHNSON
9a	PAYNE	15	WELLSTONE
9b	WILLIAMS	17	DOUGLAS
13	HASTERT	19	STRODE
17	VENTURA	22	RUMSFELD

Across: Senator Ben Campbell, President Abraham Lincoln, Bo Svenson, Tyler Mane, John Payne, Robin Williams, Congressman Dennis Hastert, and Governor Jesse Ventura

Down: Mark Calaway, Terry Bollea, Senator John MCCain, Dwayne Johnson, Senator Paul Wellstone, Kirk Douglas, Woody Strode, Secretary of Defense Don Rumsfeld

Soccer, Hockey and Lacrosse

Across		Down	
2	SONEFELD	4	WILLIAMS
4	JOHNPAUL	8	RIVERA
7a	KERRY	11	ANDERSON
7b	RUPPERSBERGER	14	SHUE
10	SVENSON	15	TESH
12a	KILMEADE	17	STEWART
12b	BRAEDEN	19	REEVES
18	SORBO	22	MEEKER

Across: Jim Sonefeld, Pope John Paul, Senator John Kerry, Congressman Dutch Ruppersberger, Bo Svenson, Brian Kilmeade, Eric Breaden, Kevin Sorbo
Robin Williams, Geraldo Rivera, Richard Dean Anderson, Andrue Shue, John Tesh, Rod Stewart, Keaneau Reeves, Canadian Parliament Member Howie Meeker

Swimmers and Rodeo Cowboys

Across		Down	
2	MCGINLEY	2	BRAD
3	CRABBE	4a	BEN
6	MIX	4b	ELEANOR
7	KENNEDY	6a	REAGAN
9	DHUE	6b	WHITE
10	PICKENS	9	MCINTYRE
11	CAAN	11	GIBSON
13	CURTIS	15	WEISSMULLER

Across: Ted McGinley, Buster Crabbe, Tom Mix, President John F. Kennedy, Laurie Dhue, Slim Pickens, James Caan, Ken Curtis
Down: Brad Johnson, Ben Johnson, Eleanor Holms Jarrett, President Ronald Reagan, Ron White, Reba McIntyre, Hoot Gibson, Johnny Weissmuller

Celebrity golfers breaking 80

Across		Down	
4	GARNER	3	WAGNER
6A	SORBO	4	MURRAY
6B	RANDY	5	NELSON
8	HOPE	7	CROSBY
11	HEPBURN	11	ODONNELL
12	QUAIDE	14	HUGHES
15A	MATTHEW	16	JACKSON
15B	RUSSELL	18	GILL

Across: James Garner, Kevin Sorbo, Randy Quaid, Bob Hope, Katherine Hepburn, Dennis Quaid, Matthew Maconnaughey, Kurt Russell
Down: Jack Wagner, Bill Murray, Craig T. Nelson, Bing Crosby, Chris O'Donnell, Howard Hughes, Samuel L. Jackson, Vince Gill

Multi Sport Athletes

Across		Down	
2	BRIX	2A	SORBO
4	CONNORS	2B	RIVERA
7	COSBY	4	BROWN
9	OSBORNE	7A	BUSH
13A	ALLEN	7B	OREILLY
13B	MAHONEY	9	REAGAN
15A	CALAWAY	12	MATHIAS
15B	GARTH	15	DOLE
19	STRODE	17	KENNEDY

Across: Herman Brix, Chuck Connors, Bill Cosby, Congressman Tom Osborne, Congressman Tom Allen, Jock Mahoney, Mark Calaway, Garth Brooks, Woody Strode
Down: Kevin Sorbo, Geraldo Rivera, Reb Brown, President George W. Bush, Bill O'Reilly, President Ronald Reagan, Congressman Bob Mathias, Senator Bob Dole, President John F. Kennedy

Athletes playing comic book characters in the movies

Across		Down	
2	CAIN	3	MILLER
5	BROWN	6	MORRIS
7	MAHONEY	10	MANE
10A	WEISSMULLER	13	SORBO
10B	OKEEFE	14	SCOTT
12	BRIX	15A	CRABBE
15	SAMJJONES	15B	HENRY
16	CUDMORE	17	FOX
19	STRODE	20	TOMMYLEE

Across: Dean Cain, Reb Brown, Jock Mahoney, Johnny Weissmuller, Miles O'Keefe, Herman Brix, Sam J. Jones, Daniel Cudmore, Woody Strode

Down: Denny Miller, Glenn Morris, Tyler Mane, Kevin Sorbo, Gordon Scott, Buster Crabbe, Mike Henry, Matthew Fox, Tommy Lee Jones

Musicians

Across		Down	
2	MCGRAW	1	ALICECOOPER
4	ADKINS	5	STEWART
6	PRIDE	6	STING
9	CYRUS	8	TESH
10	ACUFF	9	SONEFELD
11	NEGRON	10	MORRIS
12	GARTH	13	CHAPIN
15	LEBOND	14	DEAN

Across: Tim McGraw, Trace Adkins, Charlie Pride, Billy Ray Cyrus, Roy Acuff, Chuck Negron, Garth Brooks, Simon Lebon,
Down: Alice Cooper, Rod Stewart, Sting, John Tesh, Jim Sonefeld, Gary Morris, Tom Chapin, Billy Dean

ATHLETES ON THE STUMP AND THE STAGE

Soap Opera – 10 soap stars and 10 musicians

Across		Down	
3	HOGESTYN	1	WAGNER
5A	ADKINS	3	LOCKHART
5B	GARTH	5A	DEAN
7	CRYSTAL	5B	CYRUS
9	TAYLOR	9	NEGRON
10	PRIDE	11	URICK
11	SHUE	14	SONEFELD
12	LEBOND	16A	MCGRAW
16	SCHLERETH	16B	BOLGER
19	CANARY	18	STEWART

Across: Drake Hogestyn, Trace Adkins, Garth Brooks, Billy Crystal, Josh Taylor, Charlie Pride, Andrew Shue, Simon LeBon, Mark Schlereth, David Canary
Down: Jack Wagner, DJ Lockhart-Johnson, Billy Dean, Billy Ray Cyrus, Chuck Negron, Robert Urick, Jim Sonefeld, Tim McGraw, John Bolger, Rod Stewart

DR. JAMES E. HOLBROOK

Westerns

Across		Down	
2	JOHNNYMACKBROWN	1A	JOHNSON
4	HARMON	1B	WAYNE
5	GIBSON	3	MAJORS
6	SELLECK	6A	CONNORS
7	BEN	6B	TUCKER
8	PAYNE	8	BLOCKER
10	CANARY	9	CRABBE
11A	WEAVER	10	MIX
11B	OBRIEN	11	LANDON
13	DOUGLAS	12	REAGAN
15A	SCOTT	14	BRIX
15B	MAHONEY	16	STARRETT
17A	CURTIS	17	LANCASTER

17B CONRAD   18   BOND

19   MILLER   20   PALANCE

20   MONTGOMERY   22   PICKENS

Across: Johnny Mack Brown, Mark Harmon, Hoot Gibson, Tom Selleck, Ben Johnson, John Payne, David Canary, Dennis Weaver, George O'Brien, Kirk Douglas, Randolph Scott, Jock Mahoney, Ken Curtis, Robert Conrad, Denny Miller, George Montgomery
Down: Brad Johnson, John Wayne, Lee Majors, Chuck Connors, Forrest Tucker, Dan Blocker, Buster Crabbe, Tom Mix, Michael Landon, President Ronal Reagan, Herman Brix, Charles Starrett, Burt Lancaster, Ward Bond, Jack Palance, Slim Pickens

Congressmen and entertainers who competed against each other in sport

Across			Down	
4	DOLE		2	FAGERBAKKE
6	MAHONEY		5	DRYER
8A	MATHIAS		6	CAIN
8B	KEMP		10	WEAVER
10	LARGENT		13	SHULER
11	CREWS		15	HARMON
12	KIND		19	ALLEN
13	RENZI			
16	BRADSHAW			

Across: Senator Bob Dole, Jock Mahoney, Congressman Bob Mathias, Senator Jack Kemp, Congressman Steve Largent, Terry Crews, Congressman Ron Kind, Congressman Rick Renzi, Terry Bradshaw

Down: Bill Fagerbakke, Fred Dryer, Dean Cain, Carl Weathers, Heath Shuler, Mark Harmon, Senator George Allen

ATHLETES ON THE STUMP AND THE STAGE

Congressmen or entertainers who competed against each other in sport

Across		Down	
5	ALTMIRE	4	HARRIS
7	JOHNNYMACKBROWN	6	ATKINS
9	TANNER	7	NEGRON
10A	HARMON	10	FAGERBAKKE
10B	FOX	12	BRIX
12	JOHNSON	13A	SHULER
14	BROWN	13B	CAIN
16	LANDON	18	CRENSHAW
19	SELLECK	20	MARINARO

Across: Congressman Jason Altmire, Johnny Mack Brown, Congressman John Tanner, Mark Harmon, Matthew Fox, Rafer Johnson, Reb Brown, Michael Landon, Tom Selleck
Down: Ed Harris, Trace Atkins, Chuck Negron, Bill Fagerbakke, Herman Brix, Congressman Heath Shuler, Dean Cain, Congressman Ander Crenshaw, Ed Marinaro

Former athletes who have played in movies together

Across		Down	
2A	SELLECK	2A	BEN
2B	HARMON	2B	WAYNE
5	COSTNER	4	LANCASTER
6	CREWS	6	REYNOLDS
8	CONNERY	8	BOND
10A	WORDEN	10	BROWN
10B	URICK	11	JONES
12	HENRY	12	BRAD
16	SHROYER	13	CURTIS

Across: Tom Selleck, Mark Harmon, Kevin Costner, Terry Crews, Sean Connery, Hank Worden, Robert Urick, Mike Henry, and Sonny Shroyer

Down: Ben Johnson, John Wayne, Burt Lancaster, Burt Reynolds, Ward Bond, Clancy Brown, Tommy Lee Jones, Brad Johnson, Ken Curtis

ATHLETES ON THE STUMP AND THE STAGE

Former athletes who have played in TV and movies together (no comic book characters)

Across		Down	
2A	LANCASTER	1	LANDON
2B	BEN	3	LUNDGREN
4	HOGESTYN	4	CRYSTAL
		6	CAAN
8	WAGNER	7A	TAYLOR
10	PALANCE	7B	SHEFFER
12	MCGINLEY	11	DOUGLAS
		13	ONEILL
13	DERN	15	BLOCKER
16	WEATHERS	18	SHUE

Across: Burt Lancaster, Ben Johnson, Drake Hogestyn, Jack Wagner, Jack Palance, Ted McGinley, Bruce Dern, Carl Weathers
Down: Michael Landon, Dolph Lundgren, Billy Crystal, James Caan, Josh Taylor, Craig Sheffer, Kirk Douglas, Ed O'Neill, Dan Blocker, Andrew Shue

CONCLUSION

I hope you have enjoyed reading this book and hope it has enlightened you concerning some of the politicians, actors, musicians and other celebrities in which you thought were athletes as well as others that you may not have known. Although, there are others I could have included in this book, we need to conclude the material at some point and we have reached that point. If a lot of people buy this book, I will write another one, and perhaps include someone you thought should have been added to this book. Of course, as in the movies, that is an invitation to produce a sequel. While most of the material about the celebrities named in this book can be found in many different sources, I have included a small bibliography that includes some other sources where this type of information about celebrities can be found. You may notice that congressmen cited through senate. gov or house.gov was listed according to their last name. This is not a mistake. It is easier to find them by their last name. As stated in the introduction, most of the material about celebrities named in this book came from word of mouth material, public interviews, and other common knowledge sources about them. Some of the more well known former athletes are not cited. There are some interesting ways to find some of the information such as finding out an entertainer's birth name and viewing them in their sports roster. It is always interesting when you see someone in a football game and later find out they are the star of your favorite movie or TV show. There are many different sources where some of this material can be found. However you will find no other book that includes a culmination of all of this material, and certainly not the material found in the quizzes and puzzles incorporated in the last few chapters of this book that make it especially enjoyable.

SELECTED REFERENCES

"Allen, George biography". (2005). Senate.gov.

"Allen, Tom biography". (2005). House.gov.

"Altmire, Jason biography". (2009). House.gov.

"Anderson Davis biography". (2013). Andersondavis.net

Associated Press. (2010). "Fess Parker Obituary". Legacy.com.

"Ben Johnson biography". (2013). Wikipedia.org.

"Bill Cosby Profile: 1984 Temple Athletics Hall of Fame". (2007). Owlsports.cstr.com.

"Billy Crystal biography". (2013). Wikipedia.org.

"Billy Dean biography". (2013). Wikipedia.com.

"Brian Dennehy biography". (2013) Wikipedia.com.

"Bono, Mary Biography". (2005). House.gov.

"Boozman, John". (2005). House.gov.

"Brad Harris biography". (1999). Briansdriveintheater.com.

"Campbell, Ben biography". (2005). Senate.gov.

"Cast of SpongeBob Squarepants". (2008). StarPulse.com.

"Cast of Married With Children". (2008). TV.com

CBC Sports Online (2004, May 14). "Top 10 Athletes who became Politicians" CBC.CA.

"Charles Starrett biography". (2012). Briansdrivintheater.com.

"Chuck Negron biography". (2013). Chucknegron.com.

"Clancy Brown biography" (2013). IMDb.com.

"Clarence Clemons". (June, 2011). New York Times.

Coakley, J. (2004). Sport in Society: Issues and Controversies.

"Craig Sheffer biography". (2013). TCM.com.

"Crenshaw, Ander Biography". (2005). House.gov.

"Cueller, Henry, Biography". (2011). House.gov.

"Cunningham. Randy Biography". (2013). Wikipedia.

"Dan Blocker biography". (2013). IMDB.com

"Daniel Cudmore biography" (2013). Wikipedia.org.

"Dave Draper biography". (1999). Briansdriveintheater.com.

"David Hartman biography". (2009). Wikipedia.org.

"Denny Miller biography" (1999). Briansdriveintheater.com.

Deitsch, R. (2006, November 30). "Q & A: Matthew Fox". SI.com.

"Dick Jones biography". (2013). Wikipedia.org.

"Drake Hogestyn biography". (2013). Wikipedia.org.

"Domenici, Pete Biography". (2005). Senate.gov.

"Dole, Bob Biography". (2005). Senate.gov.

"Ed Harris biography". (2009). Wikipedia.org.

"Edwards, John biography". (2003). Senate.gov.

"Edward Kennedy biography". (2013). Wikipedia.org.

"Ethridge, Bob Biography". (2005). House.gov.

"Eric Cantona biography". (2013). Wikipedia.com.

Fabian. (2013). "Jake Owen". About.com.

"Ferguson, Mike biography". (2005). House.gov.

"Forrest Tucker biography". (2013). IMDB.com.

"Former Congressman Bob Mathias dies at 75". (2006, September 3). USAToday.com.

Fox News Saturday. (November 22, 2008).

"Friends of Rowing History". (2013). Rowinghistory.net.

"Frist, Bill biography". (2005). Senate.gov.

Gardiner, A. (2012, Feb). "Singer Trace Adkins reunites with Baylor's Kim Mulkey". USA Today.

"Garth Brooks biography". (2013). Wikipedia.org.

"Gary Morris biography". (2013). Wikipedia.org.

"Geoff Stults biography". (2013). Wikipedia.org.

"George Montgomery biography". (1999). Brainsdriveintheater.com.

"George Obrien biography". (1999). Briansdriveintheater.com.

Graham, B. (1999). Just As I Am: The Autobiography of Billy Graham. San Francisco: Harper Collins.

Graham, S. (2004). Move Without the Ball. NY, NY: Simon & Schuster.

Gore, Al, Jr. (2013, Nov). Wikipedia.org.

Hagel, Chuck biography. (2005). Senate.gov.

Hastert, Dennis Biography. (2005). House.gov.

Hayworth, J.D. biography. (2005). House.gov.

Heller, Dean biography. (2009). House.gov.

"Henry Hyde biography". (2013). Wikipedia.org.

Hill, Baron biography. (2013) Wikipedia.org.

Holbrook, J. and Barr, J. K. (1997). <u>Contemporary Coaching: Issues and Trends</u>. Carmel, IN: Cooper Publishing Group, LLC.

Holden, Tim biography. (2005). House.gov.

Hollywood's top golfers. (2005, December). <u>Golf Digest</u>.

"Hugh Beaumont biography" (2007). IMDb.com.

"Interview with David Canary" (2008). emmyTVlegends.org. .

"Jack Palance biography". (2013). IMDb.com.

"Jack O'Halloran biography". (2013). Wikipedia.org.

Jack Wagner. (December 17, 1984) <u>People Magazine</u>.

"James Caan biography". (2013). IMDb.com.

"Jason Statham biography". (2013). IMDb.com.

"Jim Caviezel biography". (2013). IMDb.com.

Jock Mahoney biography. (1999). Briansdriveintheater.com.

"Joe Robinson biography". (1999). Briansdriveintheater.com.

"John Payne biography". (1999). Briansdriveintheater.com.

"Jordan, Jim biography". (2011). House.gov.

"Josh Taylor biography" (2013). Wikipedia.org.

Kelly, Mike biography. (2011). House.gov.

"Kevin Sorbo Biography". (2011). IMDb.com.

Kilmeade, B. (2004). The Games Do Count. NY, NY: Regan Books.

"Kind, Ron Biography". (2005). House.gov.

"Kramer, Eric Allan, biography". (2013). Wikipedia.org.

"Kris Kristofferson biography". (2013). Wikipedia.org.

Labrocque, J. (2014, Jan. 13). "Sundance 2014: Kurt Russell goes deep for Battered Bastards of Baseball". Entertainment Weekly.

Laurie Dhue Trivia. (2009). Celebrina.com.

"Leach, Jim Biography". (2011, Spring). DMU Magazine.

"Liam Neeson biography". (2013). IMDb.com.

Linder, Z. (2012, Nov. 9). Abraham Lincoln: president....wrestler? WWE.com.

Litsky, F. (1996, April 21). "Ken Doherty, 90, Long Time Penn Relays Director". New York Times.

"Marc Blucas biography". (2013). IMDb.com

"Matthew Fox and Fly-Fishing". (1995). <u>Off-Camera with Dean Cain</u>.

"MCCain, John biography". (2005). Senate.gov.

"Mickey Rourke biography". (2013). Wikipedia.org.

"Mike Connors biography". (2013). Wikkpedia.org.

Miller, Z. (2003). <u>A National Party No More</u>. Stroud & Hall Publishers.

"Miles O'Keeffe biography" (1999). Brainsdriveintheater.com.

Mullin, B., Hardy, S., and Sutton, W. (2007). Sport <u>Marketing</u>. Champaign, Ill: Human Kinetics.

"Murtha, John biography". (2005). House.gov.

"Nat Pendleton biography". (1999). Briansdriveintheater.com.

"Osborne, Tom Biography". (2005). House.gov.

Ostro, H. (1989, April). "Prop 42, What its All About". <u>Scholastic Coach</u>.

"Peter Lupus biography". (1999). Brainsderiveintheater.com.

"Phil McGraw biography". (2013). Wikipedia.org.

"Pitts, Joe biography". (2005). House.gov.

"Politics and sport". (2004, Nov. 1). ESPN.

"President Ford dies at 93". (2006, Dec. 28). ESPN.

"Reb Brown biography". (1999). Briansdriveintheater.com.

"Reb Brown biography". (2013). IMDB.com.

"Renzi, Rick biography". (2005). House.gov.

"Richard Boone biography". (2009). Wikipedia.org.

"Rob Brown biography". (2013). IMDB.com.

Robert Osborne. Turner classic Movies.

"Robert Redford biography". (2009). Wikipedia.org.

"Robert Ryan biography". (2013). Wikipedia.org.

"Robert Urich biography". (2013). Biography.com.

"Robin Williams biography". (2013). IMDb.com.

Romano, D.G. (1972). A comparison of aesthetics, educational and philosophical implications regarding physical education and athletic architecture between fifth century Greece and twentieth century United States. Corvallis Oregon: University of Oregon.

"Roskam, Peter biography". (2005). House.gov.

"Ruppersberger, Dutch biography". (2005). House.gov.

Sanz, C. and Johnson, K. (1990, Feb. 19). "An Ex-Marlboro Man who can Really Ride, Brad Johnson Adds Sigh Appeal to Always". People.com.

Seldon, D. (1992, June 11). "Oklahoma Military Academy Alumni Gather for Reunion". NewsOK.com.

Silva. (2013). "Kip Moore". About.com.

"Simmons, Rob biography". (2005). House.gov.

"Slim Pickins biography". (2013). Wikipedia.org.

"Sonny Shroyer biography". (2013). Wikipedia.org.

"Space, Zackary biography". (2009). House.gov.

"Stachowski, William biography". (2005). House.gov.

"Tanner, John biography". (2005). House.gov.

Tarde, J. (2005, December). Golf Digest.

"Ted Cassidy biography". (2013). Wikipedia.org.

The Tonight Show with Johnny Carson. NBC.

Thorp, E. "Michael Landon, American Actor, Bonanza" (2013). ellenThorp.com.

"Thune, John biography". (2011). Senate.gov.

"Thune, John". (2012). Runners World.

"Thurmond, Strom biography". (2005). Senate.gov.

"Timothy Busfield biography". (2013). Wikipedia.org.

"Toby Keith's Biography". (2008). TV.com.

"Toby Keith Interview". (2008, Aug. 3). <u>Fox News Sunday</u>.

"Tom Chapin biography". (2013). Wikipedia.org.

"Tony Danza biography" (2013). Wikipedia.org.

"Ty Hardin biography". (1999). Brainsdriveintheater.com.

"Udall, Mark biography". (2009). Senate.gov.

Vallance, T. (1998, Jan 23). "Obituary: Jack Lord". <u>The Independent.</u>

"Van Holden, Chris biography". (2005). House.gov.

"Vince Edwards biography". (1999). Briansdriveintheater.com.

"Webb, James biography". (2011). Senate.gov.

"Wellstone, Paul biography". (2013) Wikipdia.org.

"William Smith biography". (2013). IMDB.com.

"Woody Strode biography". (2013). Wikipedia.org.

ABOUT THE AUTHOR

Dr. James E. Holbrook is an associate professor, specializing in sport management at Cumberland University, in Tennessee. He received his bachelor's degree from Morehead State University in Kentucky, his master's degree from Eastern Kentucky University and his doctorate degree from Middle Tennessee State University. As a professor of 22 years, he has written many other peer-reviewed publications, including a textbook, entitled Contemporary Coaching: Issues and Trends. Dr. Holbrook has been involved in every area of the profession. He has been a department chair, held several professional offices, including Chair for the SDAAHPERD Sport Management Council, and worked with amateur, professional and Olympic teams. He was a multi-sport athlete in high school and college, and continues to compete as a master's athlete in multiple sports. Coming from this background, he has always been interested in former athletes who moved on to successful careers outside of sport. I hope you enjoy reading this book as much as he enjoyed writing it.

www.ingramcontent.com/pod-product-compliance
Lightning Source LLC
Chambersburg PA
CBHW060450290526
45791CB00001B/49